Yes, but...
if they like it, they'll learn it!

How to plan, organize, and assess learning experiences with meaning, purpose, and joy

SUSAN CHURCH

JANE BASKWILL

MARGARET SWAIN

Pembroke Publishers Limited

Dedication
To the many gifted teachers who inspired this book

© 2007 Pembroke Publishers
538 Hood Road
Markham, Ontario, Canada L3R 3K9
www.pembrokepublishers.com

Distributed in the U.S. by Stenhouse Publishers
480 Congress Street
Portland, ME 04101-3400
www.stenhouse.com

We acknowledge the financial support of the Government of Canada through the Book Publishing Industry Development Program (BPIDP) for our publishing activities.

We acknowledge the assistance of the OMDC Book Fund, an initiative of the Ontario Media Development Corporation.

Library and Archives Canada Cataloguing in Publication

Church, Susan M
   Yes, but... if they like it, they'll learn it! : how to plan, organize, and assess learning experiences with meaning, purpose, and joy / Susan Church, Jane Baskwill and Margaret Swain.

Includes bibliographical references and index.
ISBN 13: 978-55138-211-1
ISBN 10: 1-55138-211-3

   1. Elementary school teaching.   2. Motivation in education.
3. Effective teaching.   I. Baskwill, Jane II. Swain, Margaret,   III. Title.

LB1051.C48 2007   372.1102   C2006-906375-3

Editor: Kat Mototsune
Cover design: John Zehethofer
Typesetting: Jay Tee Graphics

Printed and bound in Canada
9 8 7 6 5 4 3 2 1

Contents

Introduction

Among our main influences in the field of literacy at the time we were teaching were Goodman (1967) Goodman, Watson & Burke (1987); Graves (1983); Hansen (1987); Harste, Woodward & Burke (1984); Newman (1984); and Smith (1971, 1978, 1982).

We began our careers in education in the late 1960s/early 1970s as classroom teachers, and have filled many different roles in the ensuing years. We've worked as school and district administrators, curriculum developers, writers, consultants, researchers, and university professors. Over the decades we've been immersed in the ebb and flow of educational change, engaging with issues related to philosophy, policy, politics, and practices. Throughout, all three of us have sustained a passionate interest in literacy teaching and learning.

In particular, we have been strong advocates for the development of teaching practices informed by research. In our own classrooms we drew upon the work of leaders in the field of literacy education to develop curricula that actively engaged students in learning language and literacy through purposeful and meaningful use. As knowledge about literacy has expanded, our theories and practices have evolved, using new insights regarding, for example, literacy acquisition (Vasquez 2004) multiliteracies (Cope & Kalantzis 2000), and critical literacy (Comber 1997, 2005). Yet our core belief in the importance of meaning and purpose—what we call authentic literacy engagement—has not altered and continues to guide our work.

Based on our experiences and insights from research, we work toward the creation of classroom contexts in which students learn through purposeful language use; teachers respond to students' needs through appropriate instruction; and students and teachers engage in ongoing assessment *for* learning to enhance student success. Authentic literacy engagement in such classrooms is enhanced through a curriculum in which students are active participants, using multiple literacies as tools for exploring and making meaning of the everyday. The learning experiences in such a curriculum

- draw upon students' personal knowledge, experiences, and interests (real-world knowledge)
- bridge the gap between home and school literacies
- use literacy for relevant purposes, and build purposeful literacy events around issues that emerge
- move from learning within the school to the community-at-large and beyond
- use events to learn about sociocultural aspects of language and literacy
- integrate assessment within learning processes, using self-assessment as a means to foster metacognitive awareness.

Much of our current work is devoted to helping pre-service and experienced teachers to develop this kind of literacy curriculum.

We are troubled, however, as we survey the current educational scene and interact with many teachers and administrators. We are struck by how much of our collective time and energy is devoted to external accountability, and by the turn taken by professional conversations related to meaning, purpose, and authenticity. When we talk to teachers about creating opportunities for authentic literacy engagement, we hear a lot of what we call "Yes, buts." For example, "Yes, I would like to create authentic literacy engagement, but...

- I have to address the outcomes so I don't have time to do the kinds of things that students really enjoy."
- I have to prepare these students for the provincial/state/district assessments, so I teach what they need to know to do well on the tests."
- I have too many students with exceptionalities for a more open curriculum to work; I need a tight structure."
- I can't do that in my classroom with the number of behavior problems that I deal with every day."
- The kids that I teach need lots of basic skills—no time for the frills."
- Parents, principals, the school district won't let me do that."

We recognize that students need to handle many literacies, including those they acquire in academic settings, if they are to be successful in school and have a full range of options for further education and work after leaving school.

We've written this book for all the teachers (and administrators) who would like to create and sustain authentic literacy engagement, but struggle with how to do so in the current context. We address the "Yes, buts" directly, demonstrating that it is possible to meet the literacy learning needs of a diverse range of students through practices that are both accountable and authentic. We draw upon specific examples of curriculum projects that illustrate how teachers can foster authentic student engagement and also meet external curricular and assessment expectations. We show how the kind of practices we describe actually enhance the possibility that a greater number of students will meet expected outcomes and, more significantly, will be able to use language and literacy critically and reflectively for many different purposes.

Through our descriptions of curricular examples we address the following:

1. How does authentic learning engagement differ from typical school literacy tasks?
2. How can teachers incorporate practices that help all readers and writers use what they learn through authentic learning engagement, in order to negotiate more traditional school literacies?
3. How can teachers put an emphasis on authentic learning engagement and still ensure that they meet external curricular and accountability expectations?

We begin in chapter 1 with some further thoughts on why we believe that educators should not allow "Yes, buts" to be barriers to the creation of authentic literacy engagement. In chapter 2, we provide a framework for designing a curriculum that fosters such student engagement, including a discussion of enhancing the learning potential of external assessments and helpful frameworks that teachers can use both for planning and for keeping track of what has been accomplished. The chapters that follow (chapters 3 to 8) focus on multiple curricular possibilities: learning through the arts, activating community advocacy, developing critical consumers, working towards social justice, connecting literacy across the curriculum, and making connections between life and literature.

In each of the chapters we transform the obstacles to this kind of curriculum into positive possibilities through practical suggestions related to the following questions:

- How were learning outcomes, objectives, or standards addressed?
- How did the teacher support and extend students' literacy learning?
- How did classroom assessment practices support student growth?
- How were parents and the wider community involved from the beginning?

We have framed each chapter with two classroom scenarios. The first shows an authentic literacy engagement, and is followed by a detailed analysis of how the curricular example addresses standards, supports literacy learning, provides assessment for student growth, and involves parents and community from the planning stage. Each chapter concludes with a second example that demonstrates how similar learning occurs at a different grade level. We hope these examples will generate further thought and discussion.

We hope that the examples and discussions that follow will inspire other teachers to enact this kind of literacy and learning curriculum. We have shaped our own classroom practices through the principles of authentic literacy engagement and have witnessed the positive effects on learners. We know that schools could be doing a better job of supporting the literacy development of all learners; however, having worked with thousands of students and hundreds of teachers over the years, we remain optimistic about the potential for schools to make a difference in students' lives. We offer the ideas in this book as a powerful means to that end.

1 Insights from Research

Beyond the Reading Wars

In our view, a focus on the enhancement of authentic literacy engagement provides a necessary and productive alternative to the contentious debates that have engaged the field for many years. Literacy educators are particularly prone to construct theories and practices in terms of "either/or." There is a tendency to forget the insights offered by John Dewey (1938) 70 years ago through his critique of the human penchant to "think in terms of extreme opposites" (p. 17). There have been ongoing battles between those who advocate meaning first and those who defend code-first approaches. These "reading wars" seem to go on and on through successive generations of literacy practitioners and theorists.

The philosophical wars often play out in terms of crises. For example, in the 1980s Flesch (1985) told us phonics was the answer to "Why Johnny Can't Read." In the 1990s a backlash against whole language brought a focus to balanced reading programs that purported to address widespread student weaknesses in reading skills. Currently, a gender gap has opened up, making boys the newly disadvantaged in relationship to girls (Weaver-Hightower 2003). Documents such as an Ontario Ministry of Education publication (2004) devoted to improving boys' literacy, *Me Read? No Way*, provide evidence of girls' better performance on large-scale assessments of literacy across the world, and suggest that boys need special attention. Publishers have responded to the demand for professional books and student reading materials that address the unique literacy learning needs of boys; however, a recent critical review of the "failing boys" interpretation of achievement results (Mead 2006) provides compelling evidence that "overall achievement and attainment for boys is higher than it has ever been" (p. 4). What the data do show is "disturbingly low achievement for poor, black, and Hispanic boys" (p. 9).

Beyond the Rhetoric of Crisis

Having lived through so many crises in literacy over our careers, we resist simplistic solutions to complex problems. When we were teachers and administrators in the public education system, it was evident that both girls and boys struggle with literacy. We can cite many examples of how social class, race, and ethnicity negatively influence school success. Now, as teacher educators, consultants, and researchers, we work to look beyond the rhetoric of failing boys and to think more broadly about what might be happening in relationship to literacy education for all children and youth, particularly those the school system is demonstrably not serving well. We are concerned that so many students struggle

Although teachers cannot change students' life circumstances, we can provide learning opportunities that increase the possibility that more students will be successful in school.

with or disengage from school literacy, despite countless programs designed to address their needs. We believe that many of these well-intentioned efforts are ineffective because they are overly prescriptive and limiting, and do not take into account newer understandings of the nature of literacy and literacy learning.

We believe that literacy educators need to pay more attention to how literacy in the world outside school is changing, rather than expending energy on fruitless reading wars. We need to examine to what extent our school literacy practices prepare students to live and work in a world in which all of us are immersed in multiple forms of print and media texts. We need to ask ourselves how effectively we are responding in school contexts to young people who increasingly negotiate these multiliteracies with great skill and flexibility outside school.

Current definitions of literacy characterize it as complex, changeable, and multifaceted:

- Literacy is the flexible and sustainable mastery of a repertoire of practices with the texts of traditional and new communications technologies via spoken language, print, and multimedia (Queensland Australia Government 2000).
- In today's world literacy means—in addition to interacting with print texts —recognizing how texts are produced and understanding how multimodal forms of representation convey meaning (National Council of Teachers of English website).
- Literacy is not a set of unchanging and universal skills or knowledge. What counts as literacy varies according to factors such as place, institution, purpose, period in history, culture, economic circumstance, and power relations.... To say that literacy is socially constructed is to recognize we use a multiplicity of literacies to get things done in our lives. (Comber & Cormack 1997)
- Literacy will not be measured simply by our ability to comprehend, analyze, and communicate; instead, we expect literacy will be increasingly defined around our ability to adapt to the changing technologies of information and communication and our ability to envision new ways to use these technologies for important purposes (Leu & Kinzer 2000).

These expanded notions of literacy suggest that we need to explore the implications of research; for example, the work of Canadian researchers Blair and Sanford (2004) demonstrates how young boys "morph" school literacy practices, drawing upon their out-of-school knowledge and interests in multiple media texts. While girls may be doing better on traditional school literacy tasks, such as reading and writing fiction, Blair and Sanford conclude,

It is our contention that boys are engaging in literacy events outside of the classroom that, although not ensuring academic success, may be better preparing them for the world beyond school. The abilities to navigate the Internet, experiment with alternative literacies, and 'read' multiple texts simultaneously—morphing their own literacy practices to take up new literacies—will perhaps be more useful workplace skills than the ability to analyze a work of fiction or to write a narrative account (p. 459).

Authentic Pedagogy and Student Achievement

Our beliefs about authentic literacy engagement are informed by theories of authentic pedagogy that underlie the work of some of the leading researchers in school reform. After conducting a large-scale study of school restructuring in the mid-1990s, Newmann and Wehlage (1995) concluded that a focus on student learning through authentic pedagogy was key to improving student achievement. Reflecting on the messages of this research, Newmann (1996) states that authentic pedagogy "stands for intellectual accomplishments that are worthwhile, significant, and meaningful, such as those undertaken by successful adults" (p. 25). He identifies three criteria for authentic intellectual achievement:

1. Students must be actively engaged in constructing knowledge; the teacher's primary role is to facilitate students' active intellectual engagement in learning and problem solving.
2. Learning occurs through disciplined inquiry in which students develop deep understanding of concepts and theories through examining specific problems, using complex forms of language for both learning and communication.
3. Learning experiences must have value beyond measuring success in school. Wherever possible, students' experiences outside of school should be integrated with school learning, and knowledge should transfer beyond the classroom into students' lives.

Research such as this has had an impact on the way some constituencies have shaped educational change initiatives. For example, the state of Queensland, Australia, has focused their reform efforts on transforming teaching and learning through the New Basics Project, an integrated framework for curriculum, pedagogy, and assessment. As described by the Director of the Project, Matters (2001),

> The New Basics are clusters, families or groups of practices that are essential for survival in the worlds that students have to deal with. There are four clusters that act as curriculum organizers and are entitled, Life Pathways and Social Futures, Multiliteracies and Communications Media, Active Citizenship, and Environment and Technologies. These clusters are intended to help student answer these important questions:
>
> • Who am I and where am I going?
> • How do I make sense of and communicate with the world?
> • What are my rights and responsibilities in communities, cultures, and economies?
> • How do I describe, analyze, and shape the world around me? (p. 3)

The central features of the Project are as follows: *productive pedagogies*, defined as teacher practices that have a positive impact on student outcomes; *productive assessment*, which gives emphasis to higher-order thinking and problem solving; and *rich tasks* through which students "demonstrate their understandings, knowledges and skills through performance on transdisciplinary activities that have an obvious connection to the wider world" (Matters 2001, p. 6).

Newmann and Wehlage (1995) provide substantive evidence that authentic pedagogy enhances achievement for all students, regardless of race, gender, or social class.

We believe that there is much to learn from well-conceived, research-based initiatives such as the New Basics Project. The evidence that student achievement is enhanced through authentic pedagogy can go a long way towards contesting the belief that a return to the traditional basics is what is needed to improve student learning.

Assessment for Learning and Student Achievement

A further counter to the accountability "Yes, but" comes from current research that documents the importance of classroom assessment in improving learning. For example, Black and Wiliam (1998) demonstrate that "strengthening the practice of formative assessment produce[s] significant and often substantial learning gains," and that those gains are most significant with low achievers. Similar claims cannot be made for large-scale assessments and standardized tests (Stiggins 2004). The findings indicate that there needs to be increased assessment accuracy, descriptive feedback, and student involvement in all aspects of the assessment process.

Formative assessment practices—related to assessment *for* learning, classroom assessment, and student-involved assessment—occur *during* the learning rather than at the end of it and, as such, are an important part of the whole learning process. The function is to improve the process while it is happening, rather than to judge or evaluate it after completion. The student—as well as the teacher—is seen as a prime user of the information.

The Assessment Reform Group define assessment *for* learning as

> the process of seeking and interpreting evidence for use by learners and their teachers to decide where the learners are in their learning, where they need to go and how best to get there. (http://www.qca.org.uk/7659.html)

Most important to the process is that all students need to have clearly articulated targets in student-friendly language and exemplars of what is expected. Once these targets are clear to students, they need to be involved with developing criteria, setting learning goals, and collecting evidence of their learning. The teacher's role becomes one of giving students specific feedback on how well they are progressing towards those goals, as well as offering focused support to help them continue to improve their learning. According to Black & Wiliam, this kind of feedback can provide students with support in all three areas, the "recognition of the *desired goal*, [the] evidence about [the student's] *present position*, and some understanding of *a way to close the gap* between the two."

In addition, students are encouraged to participate in self- and peer-assessment, in which they reflect upon not only what was learned but also how it was learned, thus gaining insights into their own learning processes. Assessment for learning also involves students in demonstrating or communicating their own learning. This process of reviewing the targets and criteria, making choices about what evidence best demonstrates what they have learned, and then communicating that to various audiences (including the teacher, peers, and parents) is a complex and important skill.

Bringing assessment for learning to the fore in literacy instruction can help students, teachers, and parents to develop shared assumptions about what is important, to identify what learners *can* do, and to determine directions for the

Evidence that student achievement is enhanced through authentic pedagogy is a powerful counter to many of the "Yes, buts" that teachers raise in discussions regarding the feasibility of fostering authentic literacy engagement in contexts in which accountability is the focus.

Self- and peer assessment is particularly important for students who struggle, since it is crucial that they build understanding and confidence in themselves as learners through self-reflection.

future. Such practices make it possible to focus on complex concepts, strategies, and skills in the context of use. A focus on assessment for learning actually increases both student and teacher accountability, because the responsibility for documenting and demonstrating student learning to multiple audiences lies *with them*. We cannot think of a better way to come to terms with the accountability "Yes, but."

2   A Curricular Framework for Literacy Engagement

See pages 20–24 for an extended discussion of ways teachers can transform external large-scale assessments into authentic literacy engagements, thus enhancing students' potential for successful performance on accountability measures.

Although each of chapters 3 to 8 highlights a particular example of authentic literacy engagement, our purpose is not to suggest that teachers emulate these specific projects, but rather to demonstrate the learning potential of this kind of literacy curriculum. We give emphasis to purposeful language use and assessment for learning. We provide practical suggestions for how teachers can address external curricular expectations, document and communicate students' progress towards expected learning outcomes, and engage students actively in those documentation and communication processes.

In the chapter related to each example we provide further detail on how such engagements support the development of language processes: speaking, listening, reading, viewing, writing, and representing. We give specific attention to addressing the needs of diverse literacy learners. We show how to support students who struggle in key areas, such as

- Language acquisition
- Phonemic awareness
- Motivation and engagement
- Fluency in both reading and writing
- Comprehension
- Vocabulary development
- Use of language conventions (spelling and usage, text structures, text features, etc.)
- Critical literacy

We have witnessed how authentic literacy engagement generates a passion for inquiry and a strong sense of purpose among all types of learners. We have seen the positive effect on teachers when they have opportunities for exploration with children and for creative construction of curriculum. We know that teachers are able to support individual learners actively and appropriately within contexts that support authentic literacy engagement, basing their decisions on information gathered through effective and focused classroom assessment practices. We acknowledge and validate the many "Yes, buts" that arise for teachers when they contemplate the challenges of teaching this way in contexts in which there seems to be little support or encouragement for their work. In the end, however, we continue to believe that, as the adults who have the present and future lives of children and youth in our hands, we owe it to them to find ways to overcome the obstacles. The examples of authentic literacy engagement point the way.

Testing 1, 2, 3...

Critics of standardized measures (Allington 2001; Ohanian 1999; Kohn 2000; Graves 2002) point to the harm done to students, teachers, and public education when performance on tests becomes the primary measure of success. They draw on research that shows that when tests dominate, it is hard to sustain authenticity, creativity, and student engagement.

In chapter 1 we emphasized the importance of classroom assessment as a means both of enhancing student achievement and of documenting student progress. We share the concerns expressed by critics of standardized measures who argue that increased emphasis on testing has created a situation in which tests drive the curriculum. By their very nature, large-scale assessments can assess only a narrow range of literacy learning. Testing situations are very different from classroom and real-world contexts, in which people use language flexibly and diversely for many different purposes.

Drawing on the work of researchers such as Black and Wiliam (1998), we continue to advocate for assessment practices that research shows have the most positive impact on student learning. Nevertheless, we recognize the realities of the current context. There is no doubt that external assessments will continue to play a significant role as a form of accountability to the many publics that schools serve. We know that teachers have the responsibility to ensure that their students perform as well as they possibly can on external assessments, and that schools need to take the information from these assessments into account when working towards school improvement. In our interactions with teachers, we try to help them understand the nature of the tests being used and what the results mean. We also discuss where such assessments fit in the overall scheme of things, as one limited means of demonstrating what students have learned.

Unintended Consequences of Test Preparation

Where tests have high stakes, a lot of effort often goes into test preparation. Teachers know the kinds of tasks the students will have to complete on the tests and provide focused practice.

> In a recent journal article (Shelton & Fu 2004), Grade 4 teacher Nancy Shelton writes about her efforts to enact a writing workshop, in which students learned to write purposely, passionately, and creatively, and contrasts it with the test preparation she felt obligated to implement. When instructing for the test, her "teaching was indeed like training soldiers rather than learners and her goal was not only to help students know how to take tests, but, more important, to help them each get a high score" (p. 123). Shelton goes on to describe how the students' writing changed in the context of text preparation. Instead of exploring multiple forms in which to express their ideas and feelings, the students produced flat, formulaic writing in response to practice prompts and models of expository essays similar to those used in the assessments. Her role as a supportive and constructive teacher, reader, and responder in the writing workshop shifted into that of a drill sergeant. Students and teacher alike were stressed and bored by the pressured and restrictive approach to writing. Although her students performed well on the assessment, Shelton was left wondering what success on the test really meant.

Our own experiences with large-scale assessment have raised many questions about how best to work with students so that the results are a true reflection of students' achievement of the aspects of literacy assessed by the test. In the late 1980s, the Nova Scotia Department of Education developed an elementary language-arts assessment designed to replicate as closely as possible the instructional context of the classroom. The assessment took place over several days, giving students opportunities to produce multiple drafts of writing and to respond to reading through written reflections. At the provincial level, teachers were involved in marking sessions in which they developed and used rubrics to score a statistical sample of the students' writing.

The Department supported teachers with extensive professional development related to the assessment. An integral part of the professional development was the involvement of teachers at the school level in examining the responses and writing of all of their students.

There were many positive outcomes from this professional development; in particular, teachers involved in the provincial scoring commented on how much they learned about assessing student writing through grappling with how to score the samples. However, there were unintended, not-so-positive consequences. One of the writing tasks on the assessment was a piece of descriptive writing about a favorite place. As part of the professional development, teachers were shown how to engage students in descriptive writing prior to the assessment, demonstrating how to use the five senses to write about the look, feel, smell, taste, and sound of what was being described. The unexpected effects of this instruction were evident in the samples from many schools, where piece after piece titled "My Favorite Place" outlined, in a series of five formulaic and boring paragraphs, *How it looks*, *How it feels*, *How it smells*, *How it tastes*, *How it sounds*.

Those of us involved in developing and scoring the assessment took this as a sobering lesson about how our good intentions could easily go awry. We certainly did not intend that teachers instruct students in a formula for descriptive writing, but it was clear that many teachers, also with good intentions, followed our instructions to the letter in preparing their students for the assessment. We can only speculate about what the students learned about writing from this exercise, but it clearly did not teach them about how writers go about creating authentic and purposeful descriptive writing.

Kucer (1991) argues that it is crucial both to find ways to gain insights into students' interpretations of instruction and to evaluate school-based literacy activities in terms of the authenticity of the event. His questions are relevant today, both in terms of everyday classroom instruction and test preparation. According to Kucer, three forms of authenticity are important:

1. Cognitive authenticity: Does the lesson allow the teacher to engage students in those processes which we know proficient readers and writers use when interacting with written discourse?
2. Developmental authenticity: Does the lesson allow the teacher to engage the students in collaborative, socially mediated situations before moving to independent situations?
3. Sociocultural authenticity: Does the lesson reflect the literacy norms of the society, culture, or discipline? (p. 539)

Kucer's questions provide a framework for designing approaches to test preparation that also are authentic literacy learning experiences.

Tests as Texts

Engaging students with tests as *texts*—particular forms of written discourse—is an alternative to the "boot camp" test preparation described by Shelton. Lessons

---

Since the assessment process mirrored the kinds of literacy experiences the curriculum mandated, this professional development was intended not only to prepare teachers to administer the assessment, but also to enhance their classroom practices.

We were reminded of research by Kucer (1991) in which he critically analyzed student perceptions of a strategy lesson designed to enhance students' use of context clues in reading. Only 7% of the students shared the teacher's understanding of the purpose of the activity, 10% had no idea why they were engaged in the task, and 83% had their own interpretations, often unrelated to reading.

related to test-taking can help students gain insights into how proficient readers and writers deal with the types of texts typically found in tests, rather than simply providing practice on the tasks. When the literacy curriculum is rich in conversations about many different kinds of texts, teachers can incorporate attention to tests as part of the ongoing inquiry into how texts work.

For example, if students will be responding to multiple-choice questions related to a reading selection, they might learn how to skim the selection quickly, then turn to the questions, and then reread with the questions in mind. Multiple-choice questions themselves can be the focus for analysis of structure and language. Such instruction creates the kind of "collaborative, socially mediated situations" (Kucer, 1991) that help students develop strategies for negotiating the written discourses of tests—strategies that they can then apply independently in real test-taking situations.

The inquiry into tests as texts can include a focus on what constitutes success, making explicit the criteria by which students' performances will be judged. If students are asked to write in response to different kinds of prompts, the teacher can collect examples of each of the forms of writing students will be completing for the assessment. Then, just as an everyday classroom lesson might focus on reading like a writer, there can be exploration related to the genres required in an assessment. The lessons might follow a structure similar to the one described in chapter 3 Learning through the Arts, where students learned to write as curators.

The framework outlined below can be adapted in response to students' age levels, capabilities, and needs:

1. Read examples of the genre.
2. Identify the features of the type of writing (content, style, and form).
3. Discuss what makes writing effective (this can include sharing the criteria that will be used to score the writing produced as part of the assessment).
4. Experiment with writing the genre, incorporating the features (this could be done through whole-group or small-group shared writing, and then independently).
5. Assess examples created through group or independent writing in mock scoring sessions, using the assessment scoring criteria.
6. Reflect on how the insights related to the genre and to the criteria can be applied in assessment situations.

Becoming Critically Literate about Tests

As recommended by Stiggins (2004b), teachers should spend time talking with students about why they are taking tests, how the results will be used, and what the scores mean.

Discussions about why they are taking the tests give teachers an opportunity to help students become more critically literate about assessments that may have an important impact on their lives. The question, *How do these texts work?*, taken to a critical level, goes beyond understanding the features of the texts associated with an assessment. The question invites inquiry into how the tests, as texts, work in the world. Why do assessments developed and scored outside the classroom have such importance? Who has produced the assessment? What information about student learning do the assessments provide? Who will use this information? For what purposes? What effects do the tests have on schools and individual students?

Lessons can focus on the content, language, structures, and features of different kinds of texts, and can foster students' use of effective strategies for reading and writing texts.

Such discussions should also extend to parents, who also are better able to put such assessments in perspective when they have insights into the nature of the assessments and the appropriate interpretation of results.

These discussions can lead back to the importance of student-involved classroom assessment—in particular, communicating with others about student learning. Such ongoing communication contributes to developing a much richer and comprehensive picture of student learning than is painted through the results of external assessments. When teachers and students are able to articulate clearly how students are doing in relation to agreed-upon criteria, they become active participants in conversations about student achievement. Well-designed and -implemented student-involved classroom assessment can become a powerful means of placing the results of external assessments in perspective as one limited form of information considered in the light of a broad range of evidence related to student achievement.

Accountability: Teachers as Professionals

In her reflections on test preparation, Shelton raises several troubling questions about "success" in teaching and learning:

- Can we count "scoring high" as "success" even though the students were nearly suffocated as writers and learners, and a teacher was alienated from her own beliefs about teaching?
- Should we define "teaching what we don't believe" as a survival strategy or compromise?
- How much should a professional compromise for his/her survival in the system?
- How can we keep our ethical morals and also keep ourselves in the battlefield (our teaching career) so as to continue to fight for our children's interests? (p. 128).

We are not suggesting that the approaches to test preparation that we have offered in this chapter are perfect answers to these questions. We do believe, however, that they have the potential to transform instruction related to external assessments into more authentic learning situations than is possible with typical test preparation. Through inquiry into tests as texts, teachers can design instruction that contributes to students' insights into how texts work and helps them to negotiate these texts more successfully. When teachers and their students become knowledgeable about how tests work and what the results mean, they become part of the process of interpreting and using the information from the assessments, rather than simply receiving others' interpretations.

Taking up the issue of enhancing student performance on external assessments in ways that are both proactive and in harmony with teachers' beliefs about learning helps teachers feel and act like the professionals they are. In each of the scenarios that we discuss in the chapters that follow, the teachers responded to students' needs and interests, drawing upon their professional knowledge about the literacy curriculum, learning expectations, and language/literacy development. The same kind of knowledge needs to be applied when making decisions about how best to support students in the context of external assessments.

In addition, teachers need to understand the political contexts in which they work, so that they can make decisions with an informed perspective on the possible constraints and challenges they face. In our experience, the teachers who proactively take on the responsibilities associated with being professionals gain the respect and trust of students, parents, and administrators. As a result, they

In a context in which teachers and students take responsibility for and provide an emphasis on communicating effectively about student learning through student-involved classroom assessment, external assessments become part of a larger conversation about how students are progressing.

contribute to the creation of conditions in which they are much more likely to be able enact their beliefs in practice. In our view, returning to Shelton's important final question, such an approach holds the most promise for teachers who want to both keep their ethical morals and remain in teaching to fight for the interests of students.

Linking Content and Assessment to Curriculum

In the chapters that follow, we use examples of authentic literacy engagements at a variety of grade levels, using different organizational structures, and for different purposes. We show that these projects originate from a diverse range of situations, both student- and teacher-initiated. In addition, we demonstrate that such engagements are dependent on a solid knowledge of literacy development.

We recognize that external curriculum expectations—outcomes, objectives, or standards—differ in form and content across jurisdictions. In order to make our suggestions related to meeting curriculum expectations meaningful for all teachers, we have drawn upon the Standards for the English Language Arts (1996) developed by the National Council of Teachers of English and the International Reading Association (see page 21). This set of standards is broadly representative of current thinking about what students should know and be able to do in the English language arts.

The NCTE/IRA vision for the standards, as described on the NCTE website (www.ncte.org) is that "they are not distinct and separable; they are, in fact, interrelated and should be considered as a whole." We want to emphasize that each of the curricular examples we discuss has the potential to encompass all of the standards. We decided, however, that it would be more helpful to teachers if we provided a more detailed description related to one standard for each of the examples.

In describing the curriculum examples, we have drawn on a number provincially set expectations, showing how authentic learning experiences address these frameworks. The examples provide a model for how teachers can work with the expectations that frame the curriculum in the schools in which they teach.

Whether the project was linked to curriculum outcomes from Atlantic Canada, Ontario, Alberta, or British Columbia, the important thing is that teachers know and understand their outcomes. As you can see in the chart below, our examples, regardless of where the outcomes originated, are broad enough in scope to be accommodated in most authentic literacy projects.

Chapter	NCTE/IRA ELA Standard	Provincial Outcomes Used
Learning Through the Arts	#12	Ontario
Activating Community Advocacy	#5	British Columbia
Developing Critical Consumers	#7	British Columbia
Working Towards Social Justice	#4	Atlantic Canada
Connecting Literacy across the Curriculum	#11	Atlantic Canada
Making Connections Between Life and Literature	#2	Alberta

IRA/NCTE Standards for the English Language Arts

1. Students read a wide range of print and non-print texts to build an understanding of texts, of themselves, and of the cultures of the United States and the world; to acquire new information; to respond to the needs and demands of society and the workplace; and for personal fulfillment. Among these texts are fiction and non-fiction, classic and contemporary works.

2. Students read a wide range of literature from many periods in many genres to build an understanding of the many dimensions (e.g., philosophical, ethical, aesthetic) of human experience.

3. Students apply a wide range of strategies to comprehend, interpret, evaluate, and appreciate texts. They draw on their prior experience, their interactions with other readers and writers, their knowledge of word meaning and of other texts, their word identification strategies, and their understanding of textual features (e.g., sound-letter correspondences, sentence structure, context, graphics).

4. Students adjust their use of spoken, written, and visual language (e.g., conventions, style, vocabulary) to communicate with different audiences for a variety of purposes.

5. Students employ a wide range of strategies as they write and use different writing process elements appropriately to communicate with different audiences for a variety of purposes.

6. Students apply knowledge of language structure, language conventions (e.g. spelling and punctuation), media techniques, figurative language, and genre to create, critique, and discuss print and nonprint texts.

7. Students conduct research on issues and interests by generating ideas and questions, and by posing problems. They gather, evaluate, and synthesize data from a variety of sources (e.g., print and non-print texts, artifacts, people) to communicate their discoveries in ways that suit their purpose and audience.

8. Students use a variety of technological and informational sources (e.g., libraries, databases, computer networks, video) to gather and synthesize information and to create and communicate knowledge.

9. Students develop an understanding of and respect for diversity in language use, patterns, and dialects across cultures, ethnic groups, geographic regions, and social roles.

10. Students whose first language is not English make use of their first language to develop competency in the English language arts and to develop understanding of content across the disciplines.

11. Students participate as knowledgeable, reflective, creative, and critical members of a variety of literacy communities.

12. Students use spoken, written, and visual language to accomplish their own purposes (e.g., for learning, enjoyment, persuasion, and the exchange of information).

We would not want to mislead teachers into thinking that this type of teaching just happens. It has been our experience that, in order to provide authentic and effective learning experiences for all students, teachers play an active and integral role. It has also been our experience that an important part of what teachers do, seemingly behind-the-scenes, is the way in which they organize and plan for instruction.

The Planning Process

We believe the planning process to be organic, much like the writing process. That is, although seemingly linear, it grows and is shaped in response to the interests and ideas generated by the students and, in the case of authentic learning engagements, by the activity itself. Also influencing the process is the teacher's knowledge of the provincial/state-required standards or learning outcomes, along with a knowledge of what works (or doesn't) based on the teacher's previous experience. This might include a knowledge of learning theory or child development, of management and organizational strategies, and of the individual learning styles of particular students. Like the writing process, the planning process moves in, out, and between any and all of these aspects, as focus areas for the learning are determined, and as learning content and assessments, logistics, and resources are developed or discarded. Hence, it is more cyclic, often doubling back before moving on. See the flow chart Development of the Toy Unit on page 23 (referring to chapter 5) as an example of the planning process.

It is, therefore, important that teachers know provincial/state outcomes well and can recognize the teaching potential in the authentic learning engagements they undertake with their students. It may not be possible to know the full scope of the outcomes that will be met from the outset; however, it is important that the teacher have some idea of the learning that may be possible through the activity, to be able to plan ways in which to support that learning through direct teaching.

The planning process is also dynamic: it is ongoing and responsive to the needs and interests of the students: it is open to continual assessment, evaluation, and revision as new focus areas or needs emerge. Again, the more familiar teachers are with the components (outcomes, teaching strategies, student prior knowledge, etc.), the more creative and flexible they can be with the design.

Planning Templates

To become comfortable with the planning process, you might want to use a series of graphic organizers that help you think through as much of the learning potential as possible. As we have said, this type of planning is organic; that is, it expands and contracts as it proceeds. And it is dynamic; that is, it is responsive and changing, and continually being revised and evaluated. This process is important to document.

We have found that the use of planning templates can assist teachers in this regard. It is important to find those that are most suited to your needs. Each has a particular planning focus in mind, or has slightly different categories for consideration. We hope that these templates will provide a starting point that will assist you organize your thinking, knowledge, and resources in a manageable way.

Like a symphony conductor, who knows not only the capabilities of individual instruments and the musicians who play them, but also how the whole orchestra should perform during a concert, the teacher who has a solid knowledge of curriculum outcomes and instructional strategies as well as the learning strengths of individual students is better able to bring the diverse needs and interests of students to the fore when planning for authentic learning engagements.

The process of linking content and performance is often depicted as a series of linear steps beginning with the performance outcomes, then the assessments, and finally instruction for classroom learning. Ideally, each step is informed by the previous step or steps. In practice, however, the steps often overlap. The crucial consideration is whether classroom teaching and learning activities support the standards and assessments.

Development of the Toy Unit

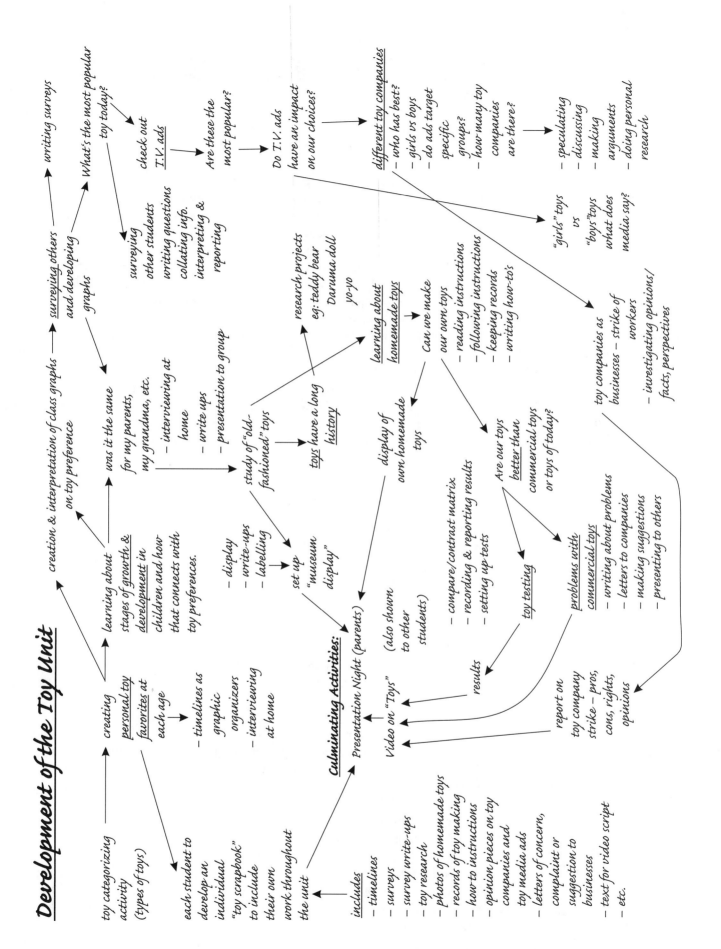

creation & interpretation of class graphs on toy preference → writing surveys

what's the most popular toy today? → check out T.V. ads → Are these the most popular? → Do T.V. ads have an impact on our choices?

surveying others and developing graphs

surveying other students — writing questions — collating info. — interpreting & reporting

different toy companies
– who has best?
– girls vs boys
– do ads target specific groups?
– how many toy companies are there?

→ – speculating
– discussing
– making arguments
– doing personal research

"girls" toys vs "boys" toys what does media say?

was it the same for my parents, my grandma, etc. → learning about stages of growth & development in children and how that connects with toy preferences.

– interviewing at home
– write ups
– presentation to group

research projects eg: teddy bear Daruma doll yo-yo

learning about homemade toys → Can we make our own toys
– reading instructions
– following instructions
– keeping records
– writing how-to's

toy companies as businesses – strike of workers – investigating opinions/ facts, perspectives

creating personal toy favorites at each age

– timelines as graphic organizers
– interviewing at home

toy categorizing activity (types of toys)

each student to develop an individual "toy scrapbook" to include their own work throughout the unit

study of "old-fashioned" toys → toys have a long history

– display
– write-ups
– labelling

set up "museum display"

display of own homemade toys

Are our toys better than commercial toys or toys of today?

problems with commercial toys
– writing about problems
– letters to companies
– making suggestions
– presenting to others

Culminating Activities:
Presentation Night (parents)

Video on "Toys"

(also shown to other students)

– compare/contrast matrix
– recording & reporting results
– setting up tests

results

toy testing

report on toy company strike – pros, cons, rights, opinions

includes
– timelines
– surveys
– survey write-ups
– toy research
– photos of homemade toys
– records of toy making
– how-to instructions
– opinion pieces on toy companies and toy media ads
– letters of concern, complaint or suggestion to businesses
– text for video script
– etc.

Planning Template I (page 27) can be used to identify specific learning outcomes, and to identify what skills, strategies, or techniques will help students reach the outcomes. In addition, it also provides a space to determine how student achievement will be assessed.

Planning Template II (page 28) uses planning prompts to help the teacher identify what students should know, experience, or be able to do. This Template can provide a timeline or pacing for the project.

The Inquiry Template on pages 29–30 provides a space in which to identify essential inquiry questions and desired student understandings. It is broken down into planning for focus areas and related skill sets, strategies, and learning outcomes. Organizing the planning with respect to focus areas allows you to teach and document specific skills and concepts—not to the exclusion of those in another focus area, but to insure they emerge at some point in the inquiry.

The Classroom Assessment Opportunities template on page 31 features assessment planning questions as related to student experiences. This template helps you consider assessment and how it will be an integral part of the project. It also helps you think about what assessment will look like as far as student activity is concerned.

While planning, it is necessary to learn the resources available that correspond with the instructional goals, student interests, and literacy levels of the students. The Resources Template on page 32 is a convenient place to record the focus area or skill set required and the resources (print or human) that will be helpful and identifying where the resource is located (Do you own it? Does the library?).

> Whether you use the templates provided in this book or design ones of your own, we hope to convince you it is important to record your thoughts in advance of and during the activity, in order to take maximum advantage of the learning potential each authentic project may be capable of generating.

Lessons They'll Like…and Learn

Organization and planning are critical to engaging students and maximizing student achievement. Being organized not only makes a classroom run more smoothly but is also important for enhancing student learning. By having a carefully and well thought-out planning process, the teacher

- maximizes instructional time
- addresses provincial- or state-mandated standards
- activates students' prior knowledge
- minimizes learning misconceptions
- places the diverse characteristics and learning needs of the students at the forefront.

In addition, classroom management issues can be minimized, allowing more focus on instruction and increasing student achievement than on maintaining discipline. Thus instruction is scaffolded, and assessments, learning goals, and content are integrated and aligned with instruction, resulting in maximum understanding.

Through authentic literacy engagements, teachers are able to involve students in topics that pique their interest and focus on their talents, and to reframe their classrooms as spaces in which learning is generated and sustained from the inside-out rather than being imposed upon the learner. The chart on pages 25–26 shows the scope and variety of these projects. It also demonstrates that both students and teachers can be the source of impetus for this kind of curriculum.

Title	Source of impetus	Impetus for change	Inquiry focus	NCTE/IRA literacy standard
The Curators Club	Teacher/colleague	Teacher develops a project to involve and interest a specific group of students	What it's like to be an artist or a curator?	12. Students use spoken, written, and visual language to accomplish their own purposes.
The Art Exhibit	Teacher	Teacher notes and builds upon a particular child's strength	How can my interest (in art) influence my literacy learning?	
Adolescent Fictions and Non-fictions	Student	Teacher overhears students heatedly discussing a newspaper article, brought in by a student, about the negative image of teens	How are teens portrayed in media and literature? Why are teens portrayed so negatively?	2. Students read a wide range of literature from many periods in many genres to build an understanding of the many dimensions of human experience
From Fighting to Friendship in Grade 3	Teacher	Teacher opens the discussion after observing bullying and cliques: "We have a problem."	What is a friend? What can we learn about friendship through literature?	
The Bed Project	Student	One student brings a problem to teacher—another child has no bed	How do we go about getting a bed for someone?	4. Students adjust their use of spoken, written and visual language to communicate effectively with a variety of audiences and for different purposes
The Town Hall Meeting	Student	Group of students go to principal about cards they think too violent to have in a Peaceful School	Should students be allowed to have cards that portray "violence" at school?	
Ashford: A Simulation	Teacher	Teacher discovers a local trip site has "No Trespassing" sign	Should we preserve a historical site: why or why not?	5. Students employ a wide range of strategies as they write and use different writing process elements appropriately to communicate with different audiences for different purposes
Equity Among Schools	Student	New student asks why they have no computer at the school	What are the factors creating inequity of resources among schools?	
Watershed Conference	Teacher	Teacher wants to incorporate a more interdisciplinary approach to learning; decides to run a scientific conference rather than science fair	How does water affect every aspect of life in Nova Scotia?	11. Students participate as knowledgeable, reflective, creative, and critical members of a variety of literacy communities
The Science Magazine	Teacher	Teacher uses student interest in magazines to reformat traditional end-of-year evaluation	How can we demonstrate our learning in this year's science class in a magazine format for other teens?	

Title	Source of impetus	Impetus for change	Inquiry focus	NCTE/IRA literacy standard
The Toy Unit	Teacher/student	Students "latch on to a topic"—toys—and run with it	What do toys tell us about the past and the present? What is the relationship between the toy industry and consumer?	7. *Students conduct research on issues and interests by generating ideas and questions, and by posing problems. They gather, evaluate and synthesize data from a variety of sources to communicate their discoveries in ways that suit their purpose and audience.*
The Crayon Crisis	Teacher	Teacher notices students' frustration with broken crayon boxes	What to do about an inferior product? (consumer action)	

Planning Template I

PROJECT TITLE _____

What are the specific learning outcomes related to this project?	Guide and Page #	On what do students need me to focus instruction?	How will parents and community members be involved?	How will student achievement be tracked?

Planning Template II

PROJECT TITLE _____

Planning prompts:

By the beginning/middle/end of this project I want students to

- have experienced…

- be able to…

- know…

What?	When?	Why?	How?

Inquiry Template

PROJECT TITLE _____

Essential Inquiry Questions What are the questions upon which the project inquiry or activity is based?	Student Understandings What are the understandings upon which the project inquiry or activity is based and on which instruction is based?
1.	
2.	
3.	
4.	

Focus Area #1			
Questions related to project focus area • give structure to the unit's inquiry • more specific or focused adaptation of an essential inquiry question	**Understandings related to project focus area** • answer(s) to focus area questions • targets a specific outcome	**Skill set/strategies/ concepts related to focus area** • list of skill set /strategies /concepts to be learned • topics suitable for mini-lessons and direct teaching	**Specific learning outcomes** • list of specific outcomes addressed by the inquiry project (use abbreviations or page #s).
1.			
2.			
3.			
4.			

Inquiry Template cont'd

Focus Area #2

Questions related to project focus area	Understandings related to project focus area	Skill set/strategies/ concepts related to focus area	Specific learning outcomes
1.			
2.			
3.			
4.			

Focus Area #3

Questions related to project focus area	Understandings related to project focus area	Skill set/strategies/ concepts related to focus area	Specific learning outcomes
1.			
2.			
3.			
4.			

Focus Area #4

Questions related to project focus area	Understandings related to project focus area	Skill set /strategies/ concepts related to focus area	Specific learning outcomes
1.			
2.			
3.			
4.			

Classroom Assessment Opportunities

PROJECT TITLE _____

Assessment Planning Questions	Student Experiences
In what ways and from whom will students get descriptive feedback during the learning process?	1. 2. 3.
How will students collect and organize their own materials and track their own progress?	1. 2. 3.
How will students be involved in developing and/or understanding assessment criteria?	1. 2. 3.
In what ways and to what audiences will students have opportunities to demonstrate what they have learned?	1. 2. 3.

Resources Template

PROJECT TITLE _____

What are the skill sets that are required?	In which focus area are they needed?	What resources do I already have (print, people, technology)?	What resources do I need?	Where are the resources located?	When will I need them? (day, week, etc.)		

3 Learning through the Arts

The Curators Club

Sandy McLean, the principal of Valley View Elementary School, believed passionately in learning through and with the arts. Under her leadership, the school became a place in which the arts had a central place in the curriculum. She advocated tirelessly for Valley View, serving a community in which many families struggled financially and a significant proportion of the children lived below the official poverty line. Over several years, the school had gradually infused the arts throughout all aspects of the school program. Not only were the arts a means of learning in all the academic subject areas, but the arts themselves were a focus, as a way of knowing and expressing ideas and emotions. Sandy actively recruited teachers who were able to provide expertise in visual arts, music, writing, and drama, and who had a commitment to her vision for the school. She and the teachers also created relationships with professional artists, who frequently came to the school to work with the children and their teachers, bringing their expertise and insights to the ongoing explorations.

Louise Fletcher's Grade 5 classroom was a vibrant place, alive with many different art forms. She frequently mentored student teachers from the Nova Scotia College of Art and Design, thus enhancing her own capacities to support the children's development in the visual arts. One of her former student teachers went on to become involved in youth projects at the Nova Scotia Art Gallery and maintained her contacts with Sandy and Louise. Together, they developed a project, the Curators Club, through which 20 Grade 5 children became artists and curators for two years, supported by the Nova Scotia Art Gallery's professional curator, who worked with the students over the duration of the project.

The nature of the project made it necessary to limit numbers, so the school developed criteria for selecting the students. They looked for children who had special interests or talents in the visual arts, and/or who were quiet or withdrawn, and/or whose home situations made access to art galleries unlikely. Louise and the principal made the selection in consultation with other staff and parents.

Once selected, the children had the opportunity to visit the Art Gallery monthly, where the curator oriented them to the gallery space and collection, and guided them through lessons related to the work of a curator. In school the children researched art and artists, and each child eventually chose a theme to explore through his or her own art. Part of the students' process of exploring the theme was finding examples of art and artists at the Gallery that connected with their own work. The children had the opportunity to examine the entire collection in order to make their selections. In effect, with the support of the

Gallery curator, the children experienced apprenticeships as art curators. Throughout, the principal and teacher worked collaboratively with the professionals from the Gallery. The art teacher, the principal, and classroom teacher supported the children's art-making at school.

The culmination of the project was a showing at the Gallery. The opening was a special event to which the children invited family members, friends, school staff, and dignitaries. The child artists and curators explained to visitors the tradition or artist that each of their own works followed, and discussed how each of the artists on display explored the theme. School-board and government officials, families, artists, and gallery staff listened respectfully and attentively to the knowledgeable and confident child artists and curators. Many of the children and their families had never before considered visiting an art gallery. The project opened a community space to a segment of the community that had previously not had easy access or felt that they belonged. The Curators Club, as part of the larger effort to infuse the arts in the curriculum in the school, made it clear that the arts, rather than being for the privileged or elite, belong to everyone.

More than one adult who attended the showing commented that the children must be exceptional. On the contrary, these were not children with extraordinary talents; they were no different from any group of children learning in any public school. In fact, it could be said that they lacked many advantages experienced by children from more prosperous communities. It was not that the children were particularly extraordinary, although the learning that they demonstrated *was* quite extraordinary. Rather, the adults who worked with them—the teacher, the principal, and the Art Gallery professionals—took both the arts and the children seriously, constructing authentic experiences that fostered the potential for learning and creativity inherent in all children. The children themselves seemed a bit surprised at all the fuss. After living and working for two years as artists and curators, they believed that the showing was a logical outcome of their ongoing enterprise. They wondered why adults were astounded at their accomplishments.

A teacher working with a project such as the Curators Club would have no difficulty documenting student learning through reference to external expectations, such as those articulated by the province of Ontario. The most obvious connection is with the Arts Curriculum (*The Ontario Curriculum, Grades 1–8, The Arts*, 1998) in which expectations relate to the production of art, knowledge and use of elements of design, the interpretation of artworks' creative work, and critical thinking. It could be argued that a good school-based art program would just as effectively, and perhaps more easily, accomplish the expectations. A strong case can be made, however, that an authentic project such as the Curators Club is much more likely to advance children's growth because it powerfully engages them in experiencing what it is like to do the work of an artist and curator. In particular, such authentic learning promotes development in two areas identified in the Ontario guide: *Creative Work and Critical Thinking* (pp. 38–39).

As **artists** children involved in the Curators Club accomplished the following Grade 5 expectations for

Creative Work

- Organize their artworks to create a specific effect, using elements of design
- Produce two- and three-dimensional works of art that communicate a range of thoughts, feelings, and ideas for specific purposes and audiences
- Identify, in their plan for a work of art, the artistic problem and a number of possible solutions
- Identify strengths and areas of improvement in their own work and that of others.

As **curators** children involved in the Curators Club accomplished the following Grade 5 expectations for

Critical Thinking

- Compare works on a similar theme
- Describe the elements of design and a specific artistic purpose, using appropriate vocabulary
- Defend their preference for specific artworks with reference to at least three elements of design

As noted earlier, the project supported literacy development in a variety of ways, and thus helped children meet the type of expectations outlined in the Ontario Curriculum for Language Grades 1–8 (Ontario Ministry of Education, Revised 2006). Although the children used all the language arts for learning and communication, their experiences with the Curators Club provided particularly rich contexts for expanding their oral communication and writing. The chart below, although far from exhaustive, provides some examples of how the project addressed expectations for Grade 5.

Language Area	Expectations Students will be expected to…	Learning Experiences Students demonstrated these outcomes when…
Oral Communication	1. listen in order to understand and respond appropriately in a variety of situations for a variety of purposes	• listening during sessions with the curator and other Art Gallery professionals and applying what they learned to their own art making and work as curators
	2. use speaking skills and strategies appropriately to communicate with different audiences for a variety of purposes	• speaking to professionals in the Art Gallery in learning situations; presenting to an audience at the showing
	3. reflect on and identify their strengths as listeners and speakers, areas for improvement, and the strategies they found most helpful in oral communication situations	• planning and rehearsing their presentations with critical feedback from peers and adults; learning how best to communicate what they learned effectively and clearly

Language Area	Expectations Students will be expected to…	Learning Experiences Students demonstrated these outcomes when…
Writing	Students will:	
	1. generate, gather, and organize ideas and information to write for an intended purpose and audience	• engaging in research related to artists and presenting what they learned in writing as part of showing art at the exhibition
	2. draft and revise their writing, using a variety of informational, literary, and graphic forms and stylistic elements appropriate for the purpose and audience	• crafting the writing that explained the artwork in forms suited to an art exhibition; using print and graphics effectively in displaying the art for a public audience
	3. use editing, proofreading, and publishing skills and strategies, and knowledge of language conventions, to correct errors, refine expression, and present their work effectively	• creating error-free writing for display at the showing and making decisions about how best to present it
	4. reflect on and identify their strengths as writers, areas for improvement, and the strategies they found most helpful at different stages in the writing process	• comparing their efforts to those of professional curators and identifying ways in which they might improve; observing audience reaction to the displays and discussing what was most and least effective about their writing

Addressing Standards

During this project, the children spent many hours learning outside the classroom. They were away from the school once a month for sessions at the Gallery and spent time at school on related experiences. In order to connect this learning with the classroom, the school articulated how the learning experiences actually enhanced children's achievement of expected outcomes.

The Club supported children's growth in relationship to many of the Standards for the English Language Arts (page 21). It was particularly powerful, however as a means of working towards Standard 12:

12. Students use spoken, written, and visual language to accomplish their own purposes (e.g. for learning, enjoyment, persuasion, and the exchange of information).

The project created a context within which the children learned to do the work of artists and art curators. Because the children made art themselves and were engaged in a lengthy apprenticeship with a curator at the site in which she did her work, authentic purposes for using oral language, reading, writing, and viewing and representing emerged as part of doing the work of artists and curators:

- **Oral language:** The children were in constant interaction with adults from whom they learned the language to talk about art, both as creators and

Sandy and Louise chose not to construct this learning as co-curricular or extra-curricular, as is too often the case when schools focus narrowly on learning in the classroom, when thinking about how to meet external expectations.

viewers. They were required to speak in more formal, public ways as part of the showing, developing greater poise and confidence.

- **Reading:** Children used reading, of both print and electronic texts, as part of their research related to artists. As they became familiar with the collection, they learned to read art catalogues and print information related to art on display.
- **Writing:** The children wrote about artists as part of their research. They also prepared invitations to the showing, wrote and edited information to display with the artwork, and prepared and sent letters thanking adults for their support.
- **Viewing and Representing:** Children learned both expressive and technical aspects of the visual arts, gaining a deep personal understanding of the multiple ways in which artists represent their ideas and feelings visually.

Supporting Literacy Learning

While the learning experiences in the Curators Club were in and of themselves supportive to children's learning, the teacher and principal had crucial roles to play in extending and focusing that learning. As well, the professionals from the Gallery and the artists who worked regularly in the school provided important mentoring. Although other adults were involved in teaching the children, the classroom teacher had the primary responsibility for planning literacy/language instruction that would enable each child both to be a successful and contributing member of the Curators Club and to grow as a language user.

Each aspect of the project provided opportunities for the teacher to construct lessons that would support the children's growth. Since the project extended over two years, it was possible to address learning needs on an ongoing basis, adapting instruction to respond to what children were trying to do at a particular time. The lessons offered included the following:

1. Reading

- When children engaged in research related to artists, the teacher worked through examples of how to brainstorm and categorize ideas and how to use planning tools such as a K–W–L chart (see page 45). She also taught them how to read for the purpose of locating and extracting information from print and electronic texts. Because the topics were self-selected and the children were eager to learn more about their chosen artists, they were motivated to learn research skills.
- Children encountered unfamiliar vocabulary related to the artists they were researching and to the technical and aesthetic aspects of the visual arts. The teacher developed lessons that focused on using prior knowledge, context, and word knowledge to figure out new words. She designed lessons that engaged children in discovering connections among new vocabulary; for example, creating concept maps and word webs.
- The children learned about text genres used by curators in the Gallery catalogues and explanatory material related to displays. The teacher developed lessons to highlight features of these texts, and then encouraged the children to experiment with these features in their own explanatory writing (see pp. 38–39, Reading and Writing Like a Curator).

2. Viewing and Representing

- The teacher and other professionals taught children to view artwork through the eyes of both a curator and an artist. There were lessons related to art forms, techniques, and aesthetics. As children experimented with their own art-making, they had purposes for analyzing the work of other artists and attempting to emulate them. They learned to "read" visual texts more deeply and knowledgeably.
- The teacher and arts professionals helped children explore the relationships between themes and forms in visual representations.

3. Speaking and Listening

- Children were always well-prepared for their sessions at the Gallery and debriefed upon their return to school. The teacher and principal engaged them in lessons in listening attentively, listening for specific information, asking appropriate questions, and using technical vocabulary appropriately.
- There were many large- and small-group lessons in speaking as part of the showing at the Gallery. These included discussions about how to be welcoming and informative hosts to the invited guests, developing a framework for what should be included in individual presentations related to the displays, drafting and refining the speeches, and practising delivery of oral presentations with feedback from peers and teachers.

4. Writing

- As part of the children's research about individual artists, the teacher designed lessons related to note-making, organizing expository writing, incorporating text features to aid the reader, revising, editing, and proofreading.
- The production of the written information for display created healthy pressure for the children to write as well as they could with as few errors as possible. In response to what she observed about the children's efforts in early drafts, the teacher introduced lessons on paragraph and sentence structure, spelling, punctuation, and capitalization. The children used computers to produce final versions of the display cards so there were opportunities for the teacher to guide their use of fonts, graphics, and page layouts.

Instructional Focus: Reading and Writing Like a Curator

The description of a series of lessons that helped children to read and write like curators is an example of the kind of instruction the teacher incorporated.

Smith (1983) coined the phrase "reading like a writer" to describe the learning that occurs through being apprenticed to the "club of writers." As he argued, readers vicariously learn about writing as they engage with texts:

> We go back because something in the passage was particularly well put, because we respond to the craftsman's touch. This is something we would like to be able to do ourselves, but also something that we think is not beyond our reach. We have been reading like a writer, like a member of the club. (p. 563)

Teachers can enhance and focus the learning that occurs by offering children insights into how the process works, and by drawing attention to features of par-

At the point that these lessons began, the children had already conducted research on artists, so they had information to draw upon in writing the explanations that went with each display.

ticular genres. As the children developed the written information to display with their own artworks and the pieces from the Gallery collection they selected to exhibit, the teacher drew their attention to how professional curators handle this kind of writing. She planned a number of different lessons that took place over several weeks.

1. Reading examples written by professional curators

The teacher collected a number of examples of explanation/background information written by professional curators. She read them with the children, inviting them to talk about what they found helpful, interesting, and effective in each. She asked them to respond as readers and potential viewers of the art. She also invited the professional curator to talk with the children about what she takes into consideration when writing an explanation to accompany art work that is on display.

2. Identifying features of effective explanations/background information

Content
- Includes interesting information about the artist's life and other work
- Places the artist in an historical context
- Helps the viewer understand the work of art, making reference to its importance to the artist and others, its themes, and the artistic forms and techniques it exemplifies

Style
- Writing is concise and to the point (viewers have a limited amount of time and attention span)
- Paragraphs follow a logical structure (main idea/details, sequence, etc.)
- Uses technical vocabulary but explains what it means
- The writer tries to include details that will spark the interest of the viewer; for example, by making specific reference to something to look at in the work

Form
- Paragraphs structured to fit limited space
- Headings, graphics, italics, and bold used for emphasis
- Well-edited and proofread (no errors in spelling or usage)

3. Incorporating the features in children's writing

The children referred back to the list of features while drafting their own explanations/background information. The teacher created a checklist of features the children could use when revising and editing, and when conferring with peers. When preparing the edited, final versions for display, the children used the examples from professional curators to get ideas for how best to format and present their writing.

Meeting the Needs of Diverse Learners

Some of the children struggled with literacy and required a great deal more direct teacher support. The classroom teacher followed up on instruction offered to the whole group by planning additional lessons for small groups and individuals. She also involved the resource teacher already working with a number of the children. The two teachers co-taught while the children were engaged in Club-related literacy activities, so both teachers were able to focus on individual needs. As well, the resource teacher took individuals and small groups aside for further focused instruction:

- Repeated shared readings of print and electronic texts being used for research, with a focus on developing reading strategies and expanding vocabulary
- Shared writing, through which students had both teacher and peer support in generating ideas, organizing, and drafting. After working together, individual children developed their own pieces—both the research reports and oral presentations—with step-by-step guidance.
- Additional rehearsal of the oral presentations, until each student could deliver the information fluently and expressively

Both the classroom teacher and resource teacher observed that the students who struggled, even the most reluctant readers and writers, were more engaged and motivated in learning situations related to the Curators Club than they had been in more school-like contexts.

Assessing for Student Growth

Throughout the two years of the Curator's Club, the relationship between instruction and assessment was seamless. The teacher continually thought through how to help children become more aware of what and how they were learning. As well, both teacher and students gathered evidence of learning and considered how best to communicate the learning to multiple audiences.

Making Criteria Explicit

As part of all of the lessons, the teacher engaged the children in thinking through criteria for their work, taking into consideration both processes and products. Some examples of the questions they considered and answered*:

Processes	Products
• What sub-tasks need to be accomplished in order to do research on artists? • What does attentive listening look like? • What strategies can be used when encountering an unfamiliar word? • What should be taken into consideration when revising writing? Editing?	• What do we look for in a work of art to discover theme or form or technique? • As an artist, how do I know that I have explored a theme powerfully and/or creatively? • What are the features of a high quality research report? • What makes an oral or written explanation effective?

* The list of criteria is far from exhaustive and changed as the project evolved.

After generating and discussing the criteria with the students, the teacher posted—in the Curators Club activity workspaces—the questions and the lists of criteria they developed in response to the questions. In conversations with the children about their work, all adults used these questions and others to bring children's attention to the criteria and to their own efforts in relationship to the criteria.

Gathering Evidence of Achievement

There were many products that provided concrete evidence of children's achievement: written representations of planning (brainstorms, concept maps, K–W–L charts, notes, etc.), research reports, explanatory writing for speeches and displays, and the displays themselves (both of the student artwork and the pieces by professional artists). The products also included artwork in progress that the students collected in working portfolios like those maintained by professional artists. The children and teacher examined this evidence in relation to the criteria that they had established for each aspect of learning.

The teacher continually brought a focus to *how* the children were learning. She recorded observations as the children were at work. As well, she and the children developed guidelines and checklists that the children used to document their learning:

- Questions to guide the research process: Have I completed a K–W–L chart? Have I developed research questions? Have I developed a structure for the final report?
- Revision and editing checklists
- Self-assessments completed after different types of work sessions: workshops with the curator, art making, writing, etc.
- Questions to guide explanatory writing: What sources of information did I draw upon? How did I incorporate the features on the list we developed?
- Audience feedback sheets used in rehearsals of presentations

The children and teacher periodically reviewed the children's documentation and the teacher observations, discussing what was going well and where changes might be needed, and developing plans for how to move forward.

Monitoring Progress in Relation to Expectations

Drawing upon all the evidence collected, the teacher was able to determine each child's progress towards the accomplishment of curricular expectations. For example, she used a range of evidence related to the oral communication expectation (see page 35):

2. Use speaking skills and strategies appropriately to communicate with different audiences for a variety of purposes.

The evidence included records of teacher observations or work in progress, comments from other professionals, student self-assessments, audience feedback sheets, and comparisons with performance criteria developed with students for specific aspects of speaking.

Communicating Learning

The public showing of the children's work to a diverse audience was the most obvious way the teacher and children demonstrated and celebrated students' learning. During the two years of the project, however, there were a number of other ways that communication occurred. The principal and teacher publicly displayed the children's evolving artwork in the school and community. Children participated in parent/teacher conferences, using their artist portfolios and other evidence to talk about what they were learning. The teacher supported these discussions with her observations. The teacher kept records of each child's progress towards expectations that she was able to share with parents and with the principal.

Involving Parents and Community

By its very nature, the Curators Club was a community-based undertaking. Arts professionals from the community were central to its success and contributed to the school in countless ways. Parents were active partners in selecting students to participate and continued to be involved throughout. The school invited parents to participate in work sessions and to view displays of student work posted in the school on a continual basis. Reports on the Curators Club appeared regularly in the school newsletter as part of the larger effort to give a focus to the arts in the school community.

The showing at the Art Gallery brought together a diverse group of adults—from professional artists and high-level government officials to parents and community members who had never been in an art gallery before—in a common cause: the celebration of the accomplishment of student artists and curators. In so doing, the Curators Club forged the kind of connections that rarely occur within and across communities, providing an example for both children and adults of the power of the arts to transcend the differences that too often divide individuals and groups.

The Art Exhibit

Asla and her family came to Canada from Turkey when she was eight years old. Now in Grade 11 in high school, Asla struggles in reading, writing, and spoken English. Well-liked by peers, Asla's friends help her with her assignments. When Karen, Asla's resource teacher, began working with Asla, she was puzzled by her lack of progress in English and assumed, like the teachers before her, that there must be a learning disability. After reviewing Asla's files, Karen learned that a number of approaches had been tried with little success. Asla's fluency, comprehension, and vocabulary were all well below her grade level. Karen decided to talk with Asla to try to get a sense of the nature of her difficulty.

Asla expressed some of her frustration to Karen in this way: "I just don't know why I can't read like my friends. I think there must be something wrong because I just don't get it. Sometimes I think in Turkish and sometimes I think in English. It just gets all mixed-up in my brain and I can't sort it out." Karen also learned that Turkish was spoken in Asla's home and that she went back to

Turkey every summer to work in her uncle's restaurant. "I love going to Turkey," she said. "I have some pictures. Would you like to see them?" Asla showed Karen a sketchpad full of images of Istanbul, her uncle and his restaurant, her cousins, their homes, and myriad other things. Asla particularly excelled at portraits. As Asla spoke about her drawings she became animated. Her vocabulary was richer and more detailed. She was more confident. Karen was amazed at Asla's artistic abilities, which had only been remarked on in the cumulative record files by the note "loves to draw."

Karen began to consider how Asla's artistic strengths could be applied to her literacy learning.

1. The next time she asked Asla to read, Karen asked what pictures she saw as she read. Asla was puzzled by this question and said she didn't see any. Karen began asking Asla to sketch the images she might see if see closed her eyes and listened to the passage being read. After a lot of hesitation and a great deal of encouragement and modeling, Asla became more skilled at this technique. Next, Karen moved to Asla both reading the passage and doing the sketching. Through this process, Karen learned that Asla didn't realize the artistic talent she possessed. She took her drawing abilities for granted; it was something she did to pass time and because she enjoyed doing it. It was also evident that Asla didn't use her strengths to support her learning in other areas.

2. Karen had Asla share her knowledge and interest in Turkey with her peers in ways that would be meaningful and interesting to Asla. She introduced Asla to a local artist who worked with her, sharing techniques and offering positive feedback and suggestions. Karen suggested to Asla that they work on a travel brochure and tourist materials for anyone who might be planning a trip to Turkey. Karen found a local travel agent who spoke with Asla about the features of tourist information and gave her samples of materials she used with her clients. Asla created maps, provided weather information, and highlighted things to do while there. She went to the Internet, as well as family members and government agencies, for information; she used photographs she had taken on previous trips, along with her own drawings, to illustrate her travel guide and brochures. She included a feature on her uncle's restaurant. Asla also put together a presentation for her global geography class, using family photos and text information that highlighted the information from her travel guide.

3. Karen took Asla to a local art gallery to see an installation by an Indian artist who incorporated journal writing into her work. Asla was very excited by the artist's work, and spoke with her art mentor about some of the techniques she saw used. Her mentor got the school art teacher to demonstrate some of them to Asla. Meanwhile, as Asla expanded her art techniques, Karen worked with her on journal writing. Asla wrote pieces about childhood memories, about her learning struggles and thinking in two languages. She wrote about the Asla who worked in Turkey and the Asla who went to school in Canada. There were Canadian images and Turkish images. Karen encouraged her to use the same strategy she employed when reading—to draw the images she saw in her mind as she read her writing. Whenever Asla struggled with writing, she was encouraged to sketch and then write. After working on the journals for several weeks, Karen suggested that Asla consider having an art installation of her own. She encouraged Asla to plan it out using the travel materials she had written, her

sketches and paintings, the photo displays, poetry, and other artifacts she had generated. She asked a gallery operator to speak with Asla, along with the local artist, about creating installations. Karen worked with Asla on a brochure for the gallery, titling her pieces and listing the media employed. Asla created posters advertising the opening and wrote invitations.

Consider This

This example describes how the arts opened learning possibilities for a much older student, showing that learning similar to the Curators Club can occur through the efforts a single teacher responding to a student's strengths, interests, and needs.

1. In what ways did Asla grow as a literacy learner?
2. How did the teacher support Asla's learning through instruction and assessment?
3. Reflecting on the learning outcomes or expectations in your teaching context, consider how they are addressed through this example.

K–W–L Chart

What I Know	What I Want to Know	What I Learned

4 Activating Community Advocacy

Ashford: A Simulation

Grade 6 teacher Brian Morse took his class each year to the site of an abandoned settlement not far from the school. While there, students could see the gravestones of the early settlers, the remains of rock walls and homes, and plants and wildlife of the area. It was a trip most students looked forward to, as they had heard so much about it from students who had gone before. On one of those trips, the students came upon a "*No Trespassing*" sign erected by a paving company that operated a gravel pit in the area. As the sign was new, and as Brian was unfamiliar with what restrictions might apply, he decided to cancel the trip and return to school, with the idea of contacting the company to seek permission to take his class there another day.

Upon returning to the school, the students had many questions: Who owned the land? What would have happened if they had trespassed? What might happen to the cemeteries that were up there, or the stone walls and foundations that they had heard so much about? Who put up the sign? Didn't the school have a right to go there, since they went every year? What if they weren't allowed to go back? One of the students said her dad was lawyer and maybe they should ask him to help. Another thought the principal should be asked to contact the company. Brian decided to continue the discussion and have the students follow up by doing research of their own. There were many ideas put forward. A number of the students volunteered parents, other relatives, or friends as potential sources of information and support, including a parent who worked for the very paving company.

Over the next few days, the students learned that the company was provincially owned, and that it had plans to expand further into what was referred to as the Ashford Settlement—but the company had not been aware of its existence. They were willing to allow the class to have their trip that particular year, but couldn't guarantee they would be allowed back the next.

The students learned that a local resident, Dave Chase, had been researching the former inhabitants of the Settlement. They asked their teacher if they could invite him to talk with them. Instead, Brian asked Mr. Chase to accompany them on their trip back to Ashford. During this trip the students learned, not only about the people and the area, but of Mr. Chase's fight to preserve the remains of the Settlement and the cemeteries there. The students were immediately caught up in the history and the local significance of the area and wanted to become part of Mr. Chase's efforts to have the area designated an historic site. Once again, the daughter of the lawyer volunteered her father's expertise.

It was then that Brian conceived the idea to involve his class in an experience that would present the complexities of the issues and would also involve community members in sharing their knowledge and expertise. He had taken part in simulations as a graduate student and thought that perhaps the technique might lend itself to this situation. He wanted to simulate the process involved in raising an issue before the local municipal council. He posed the idea to the class and they were enthusiastically on-side. The students thought they should invite the rest of the school to take part.

In the ensuing weeks, the students arranged for a suitable location off school property to hold the simulation. They decided on a local camp with a large main house and outbuildings, as it was not far from the Ashford site. A committee was struck to organize the details: book the site, designate meeting spaces, arrange for lunch and snacks, and create a set of directions to the area.

The class decided what local and provincial groups might have an interest in the issue, and asked for two representatives from each group to facilitate a group session. The groups included municipal council, department of natural resources, department of culture and heritage, the local forestry products industry, Mr. Chase and a lawyer as representatives of the Ashford descendants, the school principal to represent the school concerns, the paving company, and, of course, the press. The seven classes in the school were invited to send four participants each.

Individuals and pairs of students took on the task of contacting a representative from each group, and became expert on what each group did and their job descriptions as related to this issue. Another committee divided up the participants, including their classmates, among the groups and wrote a role description for each group indicating who they were, what their interest was in the Ashford situation, and what their position was to be, for the simulation, regarding preserving the area. This committee needed to consult with the expert on each of the groups as they wrote the description. The role descriptions were copied on card stock for each member of the group. The committee decided to color code the groups for easy identification.

Two students were designated as class spokespersons to welcome the participants, thank the facilitators, go over the agenda and timeline, and keep track of time while groups were in session. They wrote up their opening and closing remarks and also ran the wrap-up, the problem-solving meeting at the end of the day.

During the simulation, each of the groups met with their facilitators, who explained the responsibilities of their company or department responsibilities, and then led the group to plan out their strategy and write their position paper to be presented to the counselors later in the day. The counselors group examined background papers (prepared in advance) on the issue and read the letter written by Mr. Chase seeking their support and action. They also met with municipal planners, looked at site maps, and went on a trip, guided by Mr. Chase, to view the area first-hand. The media group learned about how to cover a story, write copy, and write and conduct an interview. They arranged to interview selected individuals from each group, and took photos and video footage to report on the event.

The simulation put the students in role, where they gained insight into a particular point of view. They spoke from that view, wrote from that view, and put themselves in the shoes of those with a particular interest in and view of the issue.

In debriefing sessions following the day, students talked about what they learned and the benefits of being asked to take up a point of view that was not their own. They felt they understood the issue better and had many suggestions about what they could do to get the attention of the rest of council. They began a public campaign to preserve the Ashford Settlement.

Using the British Columbia Prescribed Learning Outcomes for English Language Arts, below is a list of related specific curriculum outcomes met, and some of the learning experiences they involved:

Language Area	Expectations Students will be expected to…	Learning Experiences Students demonstrated these outcomes when…
Comprehension	1. use the information they read, hear, or view to develop questions and activities that extend their understanding	• generating questions to ask public officials, company representatives, and others, based on information they gathered in small groups or individually
	2. organize details and information they have read, heard, or viewed using a variety of written and graphic forms, including charts, webs, and maps	• creating a variety of ways to visually show some of the data they collected
	3. locate and interpret details to answer specific questions or complete tasks	• referring back to the growing body of information collected.
	4. describe information provided in illustrations, maps, charts, or other graphic representations	• interpreting maps of the area, flow charts of company and municipal council administrative structures
Critical Analysis	1. describe the purposes and key features of what they read, hear, and view	• reading letters, position statements, and other documents to determine point of view and intent
	2. compare their own opinions with information presented	• discussing and writing about how their point of view was similar to or different from that of other groups, and what the key features of those similarities and differences were
Composing and Creating	1. describe what was known about topics or issues and check for gaps in the information available	• creating summaries and K–W–L charts of the information as it was gathered
	2. locate, gather, select, and record information for specific purposes from various human, print, and electronic sources	• speaking to community members and others, in person and in writing, to obtain information
	3. identify the purpose, audience, and form for each of their communications	• crafting letters of invitation, background papers, news releases, letters of inquiry, interviews
	4. describe and use strategies for generating and shaping ideas	• determining the most effective way to influence others or gain support

Language Area	Expectations Students will be expected to…	Learning Experiences Students demonstrated these outcomes when…
Improving Communications	1. use a given list of criteria to revise their drafts	• creating error-free writing when communicating for public purposes
	2. appraise their own and others' work and make suggestions for revision	• collaborating with peers
	3. revise for content and clarity	• taking responsibility for producing their best work
Presenting and Valuing	apply the basic rules and conventions for the forms of communication they selected	• learning about effective public speaking, letter writing, news reporting
Personal Awareness	create a variety of oral and written communications to express their feelings and concerns	• engaging in debates, writing letters to the editor, giving media interviews
Working Together	1. assume a variety of roles in group interactions	• leading committees, taking responsibility for assigned tasks, following up when asked.
	2. paraphrase and elaborate on the ideas of others to clarify and extend understanding	• listening and reading carefully what was being presented, and building on these ideas both orally and in writing when creating responses or crafting positions of support

Addressing Standards

This project developed out of an interest on the part of the teacher, and was taken up by the students as a result of an actual event that had a real-world impact on their learning and interest in local history and its importance to the present-day. Events might have taken a completely different course if Brian had not been able to see the learning potential of taking up this project, and had he not been able to connect students' learning to provincial curriculum outcomes and learning expectations. However, Brian had little difficulty making those connections. Although this project supported student learning in many areas, for the purpose of this example, the NCTE/IRA Standard for the English language Arts (see page 21) that this project most exemplifies is

> #5. Students employ a wide range of strategies as they write and use different writing process elements appropriately to communicate with different audiences for a variety of purposes.

Writing became a powerful tool, through which students learned how to articulate their position on an issue and convey that position to others. They also learned to use a variety of types of writing, written for different audiences, to inform, critique, seek support, and evaluate.

Events might have taken a completely different course had Brian not encouraged his students' desire to know more about the circumstances surrounding the Ashford Settlement and the paving company's denial of public access.

Supporting Literacy Learning

In order to help students express their ideas effectively, it was necessary for the teacher to craft his lessons carefully to help students learn ways to interpret and respond to the material and information they were gathering. Using a variety of groupings, from whole-class to individual, the teacher used mini-lessons to make explicit the roles—Code Breaker, Meaning Maker, Text User, Text Analyst—the students were expected to take as readers and writers engaged with a variety of texts.

The following list, which relates back to NCTE/IRA English Language Arts Standard #5 and the British Columbia English Language Arts curriculum, is by no means exhaustive. The teacher

- used the think-aloud strategy to focus and reflect on his understanding of selected texts
- demonstrated how to make notes, to help students identify what they know and formulate questions to guide their search for what they don't know
- showed students how to refine and add to their notes as their knowledge changed
- shared his own writing, showing how to work from notes to create a letter, a report, a position paper
- demonstrated how to hypothesize, predict, read, reflect, and question using information texts
- explained how to interpret various graphs and charts, using samples the students had collected
- showed how various tools can help organize information—two- and three-column notes, K–W–L, K–W–H–L, etc.—and worked through how these could be used with the materials they were gathering
- used the overhead to show various strategies: how to read to find specific information using underlining; writing questions and notes in the margin of a text and circling key words or phrases; how to synthesize sections of the text using two-column notes under the headings *Interesting Information/Important Information*; how to determine important ideas and generate further questions using three-column notes under the headings *Current Facts/Additional Questions/Further Thoughts*
- shared his written personal response after reading a letter to the class by one of the Ashford Settlement former residents, using the two-column form again with the headings *Issues Raised in the Letter/My Response to the Issues*

Instructional Focus: Responding Using Graphic Organizers

Students often need help managing the information they gather or the ideas they generate. Teachers can help students find a frame or structure from which to create pieces of writing, speeches or oral reports, and responses to the writing of others by demonstrating the use of a wide range of graphic organizers and the purposes for which each is best suited. In this case, the lessons arose in response to the needs of several small groups and individuals working on specific topics, and to the needs of the whole class as they began to engage with the volume of information, both written and oral, they were gathering. The following is a selection of some of the graphic organizers and the uses the teacher demonstrated.

Storyboard

The teacher demonstrated the use of the storyboard when a group decided they wanted to make an information video about the Ashford Settlement. The storyboard is a sheet of paper with a series of approximately 12 rectangular boxes printed on it. Displaying an overhead of a storyboard template, the teacher had students brainstorm key information based on the notes the students had written following the interview with Mr. Chase and their class trip to Ashford. Each key idea was written first as part of a brainstormed list and then—as the group talked about what should come first, second, and so on—it was moved into the appropriate box on the template. By working on an overhead, several versions of the script could be tried and ideas easily moved from one position to another depending on their final importance.

Another group decided to create a photo essay. The teacher demonstrated how having a sketch of each shot they wanted to take would help with the overall message and effect. They developed a template for the number of photos they planned to include. The teacher showed them how to determine the key message each photo conveyed and to write it below the photo.

The teacher worked with the small group first, who became the class consultants when the need to use a storyboard approach arose.

Action/Reaction

The teacher developed this graphic organizer (see template on page 58) to help students organize the variety of issues and viewpoints of which they were becoming aware. Together the teacher and class worked through several of the issues, filling in the boxes, creating an Action growing out of their observations and then, at a later session, evaluating the results of that action.

The information in the boxes could be recorded in picture or point form, with room for a short explanation or notes, or in some cases quotes (from the speaker, a letter, or piece of text) written in the space to the right of the box.

Issue/Concern	What will happen to the cemeteries and the people buried there?
Reaction/Position	Families: Don't want the graves disturbed
	Paving Company: Wants graves moved
	Culture & Heritage: Wants proof settlement is authentic
	Forestry: Doesn't want area clear cut
Action	Make map showing graves
	Make list of families with relatives buried at Ashford
	On area map, mark off boundaries of Ashford
	Contact survey school for help with mapping
Feedback	

Venn Diagram

The teacher used a Venn Diagram (see template on page 59) as a way to visually show the issues on which groups differed and where they agreed. The overlapping circles became a ready reference as they decided how to approach each group.

Community Point of View
- wants land to belong to community
- wants area declared historical site
- wants area preserved
- wants company to stop bulldozing

Agree
Something has to be done about the graves. Neither wants to pay any costs.

Paving Company Point of View
- wants graves moved ASAP
- wants to build more roads and open more pits
- concerned for safety of workers

K–W–H–L

Early in the project the teacher, introduced the K–W–H–L organizer (see template on page 60) as a way for students to examine their own prior knowledge and to use to plan for future research. He demonstrated how this chart could be used as an aid prior to, during, and after reading some of the research materials they were collecting.

K	W	H	L
What we already <u>K</u>now	**What we <u>W</u>ant to know**	**<u>H</u>ow we plan to find out**	**What we have <u>L</u>earned**
There was a settlement at Ashford in the 1800s.	Why did people settle there? What did they do? Was there a school?	Check in Library. Check with Mr. Chase.	To work in the woods and the lumber mill.
There are two graveyards.	Who is buried there? Who is the youngest person buried there? How old? Who is the oldest? How old?	Go to cemeteries and make a list. Ask Mr. Chase.	8 in one cemetery 12 in the other. Youngest was a baby—no age. Oldest was 54.
Ashford Settlement is abandoned.	What happened to the people? Why did they leave?	Check Library documents. Interview Mr. Chase.	No more wood. Land not good enough to grow crops—too rocky.

A variation on K–W–H–L is the K–W–L organizer (see page 45).

Chain of Events

Organizing events and actions was a big part of this project, and having a way to keep track and organize these activities was particularly important. The teacher showed students how to use a Chain of Events template (see page 61) to describe the stages of an event, the actions of a group or individual, or the steps in a procedure. Simply a chain of boxes in which to record the information in sequence, this tool helps students answer the following questions:

- What is the first step in the procedure or initiating event?
- What are the next stages or steps?
- How does one event lead to one another?
- What is the final outcome?

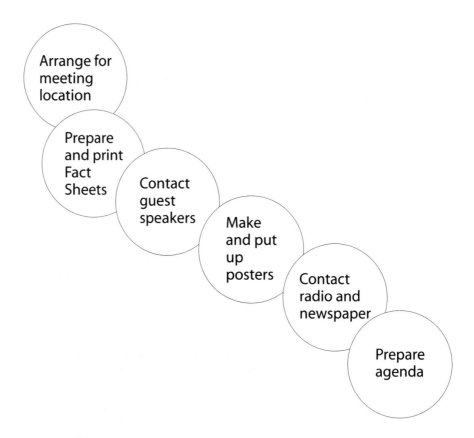

The teacher and students used these organizers and others; they also modified common ones to suit their own needs and purposes. They quickly had a large selection from which to choose for other projects.

Meeting the Needs of Diverse Learners

The teacher used graphic organizers to provide important support for students who were struggling with reading and writing. Organizers help these students work with information in manageable chunks. Since they are also ideal for adding drawing to the recording process, they provide built-in prompts for less-proficient readers, giving them a greater degree of independence and self-confidence.

Assessing for Student Growth

Brian was especially concerned about evaluating students during the Ashford Settlement project. He decided to involve his students in the creation and use of rubrics to assess and evaluate their performance in a variety of areas, as they were already familiar with the use of rubrics as part of the approach to students' writing he had been using.

Before going beyond the initial discussion phase of the project, Brian raised this issue with his students. He talked to them about the need to document their growth and showed them how applying rubrics to various aspects of their work on this project would be a useful tool for describing the knowledge and skills a particular activity required, based on a specific set of performance criteria. They agreed to develop the performance criteria together, and to use those criteria to create a self-assessment checklist to help them monitor and assess their own work. Each rubric contained the Key Elements that make up each task evaluated and the accompanying Evaluative Criteria. Below is a sample of the rubric used to evaluate student-developed Fact Sheets for Ashford Settlement:

Key Elements	Evaluative Criteria
Accuracy/Comprehension	The writing demonstrates understanding of the information, based on a variety of sources. The information is accurate and appropriate to the topic.
Ideas	Ideas are relevant and developed clearly.
Organization	The writer shows an understanding of the Fact Sheet format and has organized the information in a concise way.
Language	Tone, voice, and word choice is appropriate for an information Fact Sheet.
Mechanics	The writing uses the conventions of language accurately with few errors.
Scoring Levels	All Key Elements are evident 3 to a high degree 2 to a satisfactory degree 1 to a limited degree

By developing the Key Elements and Evaluative Criteria together, students had a clear understanding of what was expected. It helped them be more focused on the task and gave important ongoing individual feedback.

Involving Parents and Community

Parents and community members were involved directly in the simulation as resource persons and facilitators, and as audience members and invited guests during information nights and presentations. An information sheet outlining the project and seeking participation went home to each household. Parents were asked if they were willing to share information or particular skills. Some parents donated artifacts from the Ashford Settlement, such as photographs, letters, old deeds, and newspaper articles. Others volunteered to help students expand their computer skills or as research contacts. There were many opportunities for parents and community to become involved, not only during the lead up to the simulation but also during and after. By its very nature, this topic was of interest to many and had wide appeal to parents and grandparents. They were very supportive of the students' efforts and were proud of the action they were taking to organize the community in an effort to preserve a local heritage site.

Equity Among Schools

Northfield Town School was originally built around 1880 and is one of the oldest schools in Canada. Like many older schools, it does not have a gym, so the students travel across town to another facility, reducing teaching time by 90 minutes each week. The school does not have a lot of new equipment, but its high ceilings, archways, and large classrooms have a lot of architectural charm.

Steve, a Grade 12 student, transferred from Ottawa into Northfield and was in Marla Schwartz's history class. Steve immediately questioned why Northfield didn't have a gym or computer equipment. Steve's questioning led Marla and the class to analyze their school in relation to other district schools, and to pose questions regarding the current state of affairs. After a lot of discussion, with students conveying a range of opinions on the quality of their education, along with some disagreement on the facts, Marla suggested that perhaps they might be interested in an inquiry project to determine just what the actual situation was between their school and others in the district.

Together they brainstormed the issue using the four-column K–W–H–L format (see template on page 61), to decide what they already knew, what they wanted to find out, how they might find out what they wanted to know, and what they learned. From this they also generated a series of inquiry questions:

- When school board people use the term "equity among schools" what do they mean?
- What criteria do students of Northfield think makes up a really good school?
- Is this the same criteria of students in other schools would use?
- How do these schools measure up to students' criteria?
- If there are differences among schools, why is that?
- Who makes these decisions?

They made a list of the work that needed to be done and divided into groups based on interests and expertise or access to specific contacts or information. One group inventoried school facilities. Another wrote, distributed, and collated student surveys. Another contacted other schools with a variation of the first survey and collated the results. Yet another group looked into who makes the decisions regarding school facilities and equipment. They interviewed the principal, other teachers, the school board chair, the local MLA (provincial representative), and some parents.

Each committee worked on a report and a presentation based on their findings. They had found that students, despite the lack of equipment and the old facilities, felt their school was a great school based on the criteria they had established, which included ample space in which to work and friendly, supportive teachers. Next they contacted the principals of the other participating schools to ask for feedback on the draft of their report. The asked if a class in the school might send them some photos to illustrate the points made. The Northfield students also asked for any suggestions or feedback on their document and informed the schools they were hosting an information night at Northfield.

In preparation for that night, the students distributed the final report to the school staff. They invited municipal officials, department of education authorities and school board members, parents, community members, staff, and the press to the presentation. Each committee created a PowerPoint™ presentation with photos and video footage to illustrate their points, including the photos from the other participating schools. The student inquiry was an eye-opener for parents and community members alike. The students ended the night by seeking volunteers from the various sectors to form a committee to develop an action plan and to seek solutions to the equipment and facility needs the students presented.

Consider This
1. What was the source of impetus for this project?
2. How did this classroom project help the students and the broader community see themselves differently?
3. In what ways did students use multiple forms of literacy to explore issues and take action?

Action/Reaction Graphic Organizer

Issue/Concern	
Reaction/Position	• • • • •
Action	
Feedback	

Venn Diagram

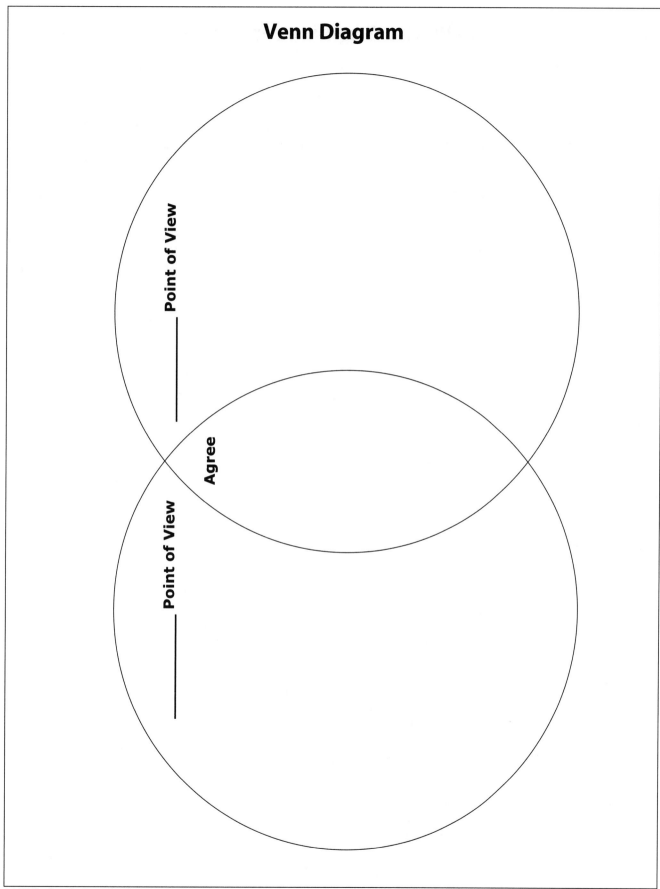

Point of View _____

Agree

Point of View _____

K–W–H–L Graphic Organizer

K	W	H	L
What we already Know	**What we Want to know**	**How we plan to find out**	**What we have Learned**

Chain of Events Graphic Organizer

5   Developing Critical Consumers

The Toy Unit

As part of a class activity on categorizing, Olivia Reid's Grade 4 students brainstormed lists of different toys and then grouped them into categories. During the process, students made comments like "Oh, I had one of those when I was four," or "In daycare, I always rode on the red truck." Responding to the children's comments, Olivia asked her students to think about what their favorite toy at each age was. With their parents' help, each child listed a special toy they had at each age and wrote about why it had been their favorite. They used this information to create a personal Toy Timeline.

The class then compiled their lists and developed class graphs for each age, with toys represented in categories. They discussed the results, considering the various stages of early childhood development and how different toys might interest a child at different stages. For example, they concluded that the favorite toy category at age two was *stuffed toys* because "Two year olds like to squeeze and chew and sleep with them. It makes them feel better to hug something." The compiled class data went into a class Toy Book.

With the students' interest in toys piqued, they went on to research the toys their parents had loved. They began to research the history of toys, using the library and online resources. They checked out the local historical museums. They collected photos and examples, set up a class display, wrote about the toys, and even played with them. Students discovered that many toys—like the yo-yo, which started out as a weapon—have long and interesting histories. Throughout the unit, a favorite activity was making some of the toys. One student discovered that a popular young child's toy, the Weeble® (a small roly-poly doll with no appendages that can be pushed over and rocks back up) was actually a modern version of an ancient Japanese Daruma doll, which in turn represented the story of a holy man who meditated so long his legs shriveled up. They discovered that traditional Daruma dolls were made by hand and that, as Japanese girls and boys would paint their own dolls, they would paint one eye, make a wish, then paint the other when the wish came true. In addition to making their own Daruma dolls, some students became interested in learning more about Buddhism, and others researched the toy company that had used the idea of the Daruma to develop and sell Weebles®.

In researching the company who made Weebles®, they discovered many familiar toys made by the same company. Students started making lists of toys and the companies that made them. A group of students were interested in toy advertisements on television—especially those shown during Saturday-morning cartoons or after-school kids' specials. They developed a Saturday-morning toy ad survey : they asked their classmates to watch TV on a Saturday morning and list what toy ads were shown, what toy companies sponsored the ads, the number of times an ad was shown, and a brief description of the ad. The following Monday, the teacher and students had a discussion about the ads, their frequency, and the messages they were giving to the children.

At the same time, one student discovered newspaper articles about a workers' strike at a national toy company—one in support of the toy company and one outlining the workers' perspective. Several students investigated the company in more depth, discovering that it was a parent company for five large, seemingly independent toy companies. Looking back at their Saturday-morning toy ad data, they realized that all the ads, while appearing to be representing different companies, were controlled by the same parent company. Further, they discovered that the workers— mostly immigrants making minimum wage with no benefits—were striking for safer and healthier working conditions. They also found out that the company had been cited in the past with numerous health and safety violations. During the daily meeting time, a number of students expressed their growing sense of upset with the behavior of the toy company. They wanted to be able to express their opinions and feelings.

As a whole-class group, the teacher and students talked about different ways that people (citizens) can express their concerns and feelings. They decided to write letters of complaint to the company and letters of support for the workers, and to develop a videotaped news report about the toy industry for the school video system. In addition to information and analysis from the toy ad surveys and some interesting toy histories, the report would include a section on the labor dispute, the issues of the workers, and the profit margins of the company. The teacher and students explored ways to express a concern both in writing and in speaking, and the effects that different ways of wording a concern can have on the audience

Another group of students started comparing toys—their quality, durability, and price—as well as examining the kinds of problems they personally had encountered with certain toys. They made comparisons, decided which toys were the best value, and presented their information to the whole group. These findings were also included in the Toy Report for the newscast. Still others wrote up their complaints and concerns about specific toys, made suggestions for improvements, and sent the letters to the toy manufacturers, often receiving responses from the companies.

As the chart below indicates, many of the learning outcomes in different subjects are closely related. Using the British Columbia Prescribed Learning Outcomes for English Language Arts (Grade 4) and for Social Studies (Grade 4) as an example, specific student experiences or activities are shown to address a number of these outcomes in both subjects.

British Columbia Department of Education English Language Arts and Social Studies Learning Outcomes (Grade 4)	Related Student Experiences
ELA: describe and recount key ideas or information from various media SS: locate and record information from a variety of sources	Students recorded information from watching TV toy ads, as well as catalogue and magazine toy ads.

British Columbia Department of Education English Language Arts and Social Studies Learning Outcomes (Grade 4)	Related Student Experiences
ELA: demonstrate an awareness of relationships among the elements of story structure, including plot, setting, and characters • interpret their impressions of simple and direct stories, poetry, other print material, and electronic media	Students recorded and analyzed the toy ads in terms of setting, characters, and action, and interpreted the messages both stated and implied to the audience.
ELA: organize information or ideas they have read, heard, or viewed in the form of simple charts, webs, or illustrations SS : organize information into a presentation with a main idea and supporting details • demonstrate understanding of timelines	Students created their own personal toy timelines with explanations, as well as developing class toy timelines, bar and line graphs to represent their data. They also created a variety of displays of actual toys and information (posters, bulletin boards, class books) about toys for the classroom.
ELA: relate the works they hear, view, or read to their personal experiences or to other works	Teacher read several grade-appropriate novels to the students and talked about how the characters' experiences with toys were similar or different to the students' own experiences.
ELA: identify the purpose of and audience for oral, written, and visual communications • share what they know about chosen topics • create and present a variety of personal and informational communications, including written and oral poems, stories, explanations, informal oral reports and dramas, personal letters, and illustrated charts or posters	Students presented information or ideas to each other, to the teacher, to parents, to toy companies, to schoolmates. They developed written reports, oral presentations, demonstrations, scrapbooks, video reports, and formal letters. Throughout the project, the teacher helped the students to be aware of the different needs of each audience as well as the purpose of each presentation—to amuse fellow students, to interest parents, to inform companies, to express an opinion, etc.
SS: identify and clarify a problem, issue, or inquiry	See page 66 for questions, inquiries, and problems listed under Learning Experiences connected to NCTE/IRA Standard #7.
SS: locate and map world continents and oceans using simple grids, scales, and legends	Throughout the project, students discovered toys or issues relating to children in other countries. As they talked about these places, they made reference to a large map displayed on the wall. Around the map, they posted brief descriptions of the toys or toy issues from that area. For example, they wrote up a brief about the yo-yo and located the Philippines; they marked the countries that the immigrant workers at the toy company came from; etc.
SS: assess at least two perspectives on a problem or issue, in the past and in the present	Students explored the issues around a strike at a toy company from the perspectives of the company and the workers, and developed a report to be presented to other students.

Addressing Standards

Since the central topic of this unit—toys—is not a part of any specific curriculum guide, it was important that parents and school administrators could see how the work was addressing the learning outcomes. Uninformed visitors to the class would see many students making and playing with toys as well as engaged in writing, reading, talking, and even arguing with each other. Therefore, the teacher was careful to articulate clearly the learning expectations for the students. Like the other projects in this book, aspects of the Toy project can be seen to address most of the NCTE/IRA Standards for the English Language Arts (see page 21), but the standard that the project most exemplified was

> 7. Students conduct research on issues and interests by generating ideas and questions, and by posing problems. They gather, evaluate and synthesize data from a variety of sources (e.g., print and non-print texts, artifacts, people) to communicate their discoveries in ways that suit their purpose and audience.

The topic, although not prescribed by any curriculum guide for a Grade 4 class, allowed the students to become passionately involved in all aspects of this standard.

NCTE/IRA English Language Arts Standard #7	Learning Experiences
Students conduct research on issues and interests by generating ideas and questions…	Students asked and investigated the following questions (a sample): • What were my favorite toys at age 1, 2, 3, and so on? • Did my parents have similar toy favorites when they were children? • Why do two-year-old children seem to like stuffed toys best? • How come games become more and more popular after the age of 5? • Do children in other countries (cultures) like different toys? • How do the toy companies invent new toys? • Why are there so many toy ads on TV on Saturday morning? • How come there are so many different toy companies? • Why are the toy company workers striking? • How come some toys break easily? • What will toys of the future look like? Students constructed many toys, reading the instructions, recording their progress, working out any problems, and sharing the results with classmates.
…and by posing problems.	How can we find out what the most popular toy was at a certain age? • interviews at home, compilation of data, creation of graphs

NCTE/IRA English Language Arts Standard #7	Learning Experiences
...and by posing problems. (cont'd)	How can we express our concerns to the toy companies? • write letters How can we find out about children's toys in other countries? • using research books, collecting artifacts, Internet sites, museum visits Which toy (different brands) is better (stronger, lasts longer, has less breakdowns, etc)? • toy testing, developing criteria for comparison
They gather, evaluate and synthesize data...	Students gathered information about their own and their parents' toy preferences by talking to and interviewing family members. Students collected and collated the toy favorites data, looked for trends and themes, and speculated on reasons. Students conducted a survey of toy ads during the Saturday-morning TV shows.
...from a variety of sources (e.g. print and non-print texts, artifacts and people)...	Students used primary sources—parents, family members, and community members—to interview or have as guests in their classroom. Students collected and studied artifacts (old toys from family or community). Students researched using reference books, websites, magazines, craft books, newspapers, television programming.
...to communicate their discoveries in ways to suit their purpose and audience.	Students prepared individual toy scrapbooks to chronicle their own toy histories, as well as what they learned about toys, toy-making, and the toy industry. Student scrapbooks were used to demonstrate their learning during the project to teacher and parents. Students set up displays of and about toys to inform their parent audience. Students wrote letters of concern or complaint to toy companies, expressing their opinions and experiences. Students developed a video of a Toy Report —giving information, expressing opinions, and entertaining their schoolmates.

Students never lacked for questions and speculation, as they investigated a topic they felt comfortable with and yet were still eager to know more about.

In this project, students were involved in researching topics of personal interest. They used many sources of information including their own experiences. Students were excited to uncover unexpected connections between toys and history, the world of television, business, psychology, and other fields of adult endeavors. In addition, students, in discussions with the teacher, became more aware of how different people use language for different purposes.

Supporting Literacy Learning

Since students held very strong opinions on many issues that arose —toy advertising, toy company workers, durability of toys, age/ favorites—the teacher focused on ways to support the students as they gathered, interpreted, and presented information as part of forming and expressing opinions.

Throughout this project, students increased their understanding of how language is used to analyze, manipulate, inform, and express opinions. From television ads to newspaper articles, from talking to their parents to reading informational texts, the students collected and reflected upon how the experiences of others fit with their own experiences with toys. While the topic of toys was both familiar and enjoyable, the teacher used the interest of the students to explore in detail the reading and writing of factual material.

Instructional focus: Factual Writing

Writing from Graphs and Charts

> • interpret their impressions of simple and direct stories, poetry, other
>   print material, and electronic media

Using the compiled class data on favorite toys as an example, the teacher led a discussion about interpreting and writing based upon information from a graph. Each student wrote up their reasoning for the age-favorite graphs and the popularity-over-time graphs. The students then shared and discussed the different reasons based upon the data and their own experiences.

> The favorite toy at age four was the push/pull toy. I think a lot of boys would have put that down because most of them had trucks. (Chris)

> The favorite toy at age eight was games. Most boys and girls were getting bored with dolls and wanted something more exciting to play with. (Taj)

After writing up the data from the compiled class graphs, the students then wrote up their own toy-favorites graph. For those needing support, the teacher provided a template to use in writing:

> "When I was ____, my favorite toy was _____. It (describe the toy). It was my favorite toy because _____."

> When I was one, my favorite toy was a dog that looked like Snoopy. It was black and white. I used to lug it around everywhere. I got it for Christmas from a friend of the family. I liked it because it was so cute and cuddly. (Jill)

> When I was three, I got a red plastic tractor that you could peddle. I used to hook my wagon onto my tractor and my sister would pull me around in it. I got it in Germany and you can't get them that big here. It could hold two people. (Kurt)

Creating a Factual Report

> • create and present a variety of personal and informational communications, including written and oral poems, stories, explanations, informal oral reports and dramas, personal letters, and illustrated charts or posters

Toy-making problems were shared and suggestions for improvement came from the group. Students would give their toy-making forms to another student to see if they could follow the instructions and make the same toy.

The teacher provided many toy-making resources: in books and magazines, from various websites. Students were encouraged to find a toy they might like to make, read the instructions, collect the materials, and make the toy. After completing it, they would fill out a form (see Toy-Making Report on page 73) to put into their Toy Scrapbooks and to help them present their project to groups of other students.

Filling out Forms

> • describe and recount key ideas or information from various media

The teacher used the opportunity to use and talk about words—such as setting, characters, action—and elements they had been looking at in their stories.

Before filling out the forms, the teacher had led the students in a discussion of what information they wanted about Saturday-morning TV toy ads, and together they decided the questions and ways to record the information. Taking their suggestions, the teacher made up forms for the students to use at home (see Toy Advertising Survey on page 74).

After completing the forms, the teacher and students discussed whether the forms made it easier or more difficult to collect information. They also discussed what worked well about the forms and what could be changed to make them better.

Meeting the Needs of Diverse Learners

This project created an extremely supportive context for all the learners in the class. The topic was connected to the children's lives outside of school; every one of them, whatever the academic abilities or learning needs, could draw upon extensive prior knowledge about toys to contribute to the group enterprise. Children could participate in many ways, not only through reading and writing a range of texts, but also through contributing photos and concrete examples, and demonstrating their knowledge through hands-on experiences and visuals. A variety of forms of whole-class and small-group work encouraged collaboration. The teacher organized group activities so that children with different strengths and needs could support each other. She also developed templates and forms that provided structures for recording information and writing. While helpful to all the children, these were particularly important for children who struggled with literacy.

Assessing for Student Growth

Students kept their folders with them during class time, then returned them to a central location at the end of the day so the teacher could peruse them as she had time.

In a project such as this, with students involved in many different aspects of the same topic, it is important that the students themselves are involved in collecting and collating evidence of their own learning.

During the project, students kept all their work in special work folders. Inside each folder, the teacher had stapled a feedback sheet, where she could write comments, suggestions, or a request to meet with the student. Each student was also responsible for developing a Toy Scrapbook, in which they presented their personal information, class data, interesting discoveries, research questions, and a record of any action they took. As in any portfolio, students could choose what to include in their personal Toy Scrapbook. Students were encouraged to find interesting ways to present their information and were given regular opportunities to work on their scrapbooks, share their progress, and offer feedback to each other. Some students included one or more of the feedback forms as a way to show that they had used the advice of their classmates to improve their work and show growth.

During the sharing suggestions, students would use a Two Stars and a Wish (see page 75) response, either oral or written.

The individual scrapbooks were used by the students, first to reflect upon their own learning, and then to demonstrate what they had learned to their classmates, to the teacher, and finally to their parents. The teacher posed several questions to help the students focus their learning.

- What did you learn about toys and yourself?
- What did you learn about toy-making?
- What ways did you use to find out information about toys and the toy industry?

Before the session with parents, Olivia had the students write a self-assessment, demonstrating how they addressed four learning outcomes by referring to specific evidence in their Scrapbook:

- I can find out about topics or questions that interest me.
- I can gather information from different sources.
- I can present my information in different ways.
- I can present my work to different audiences.

The self-assessment was included in the Toy Scrapbook to be discussed with the parents.

To wrap up the unit, students held a special evening session: the classroom was filled with the toy displays they had created; they showed their Toy Report video; and each child shared their Toy Scrapbook with a parent or adult friend. During the session with parents, students showed their Scrapbooks, focusing on what they learned about toys and what they learned about themselves as learners. Forms were provided and parents were encouraged to write a response to their children's work using Two Stars and a Wish (see page 75), either that evening or later at home.

Involving Parents and Community

Parents/guardians were involved from the first in this project. Students asked parents, grandparents, and older siblings about the toys they had played with as children. Many families got out old photos and shared family stories of "that old red bear your Great-grandma gave you." Parents and students enjoyed reminiscing and speculating on the reasons certain toys were favorites. A number of parents came into class to show how to make certain kinds of toys or to assist during the make-it sessions. Others offered to lend or bring in and talk about toys from the past. Family members were amused and interested to see their children "analyzing" toy ads on Saturday-morning TV and, since this unit was only a few months before Christmas, many took an interest in the toy-testing the students conducted. At the end of the unit, family members became the audience for which the students prepared their toy displays and individual scrapbooks.

The Crayon Crisis

Crayons, markers, and other school supplies are items with which primary children are readily familiar. Roberta Bailey's five-year-olds were no exception. She loved to watch their eager faces as they took their school supplies out on the first day of school and put them into their storage trays. However, without fail, by the time students had used their markers or crayons for the first time and begun the clean-up ritual, those eager faces would turn from smiles to frustration. Just as the box was almost full, the bottom would open and the markers or crayons would spill over the floor. Roberta had tried suggesting that the markers be taken out of the box and be stored in a tray, or that the bottom of the boxes be taped. Although some of the children took her up on these suggestions, most liked the original boxes and couldn't understand why they couldn't master the art of putting all the crayons or markers back in the box—just as they had looked when brand-new.

Several months into the school year, the children were learning about the rainforest and doing lots of art projects so they could turn their room into a rainforest. The crayon and marker situation reached crisis proportions. Near the end of a busy afternoon of creating replicas of some of the tropical plants found in the various layers of the rainforest, time had somehow gotten away from Roberta, who usually made sure there was ample for the children to clean up without worrying about missing their bus. Art supplies were strewn everywhere when, suddenly realizing it was almost bus time, Roberta announced it was time to quickly clean up. The children sprang into action. All was going well until the all-too-familiar sound of crayons falling to the floor was heard. As Roberta hurried to help, another box gave way and markers cascaded to the floor amidst the cries of a tired and frustrated five-year-old. This scene was repeated five or six times, until a boy named Charlie cried out, "Why can't somebody do something about these boxes!" Indeed, thought Roberta, and she vowed to start the next morning's sharing with Charlie's comment, providing the opportunity for the children to be that "somebody."

The next morning Roberta engaged the children in a reflection on their disastrous clean-up experience. They talked about how they felt, how they had tried to help, and what they thought about the way the art materials were packaged. They talked about where and how the crayons and markers were made.

Roberta had a book about the making of crayons: the pictures showed the boxes being made by a machine and the crayons being put inside, again by machine. She also was able to get permission to show a short segment on markers from a TV show that explains how things are made. Again, the boxes were shown being put together, but this time a person was shown checking the quality of the work. Mark thought that the person checking should not only check that all the markers were in the box, but should also check the boxes themselves. Karen said they probably did. Anna suggested that maybe the company people didn't know the problems kids have with their boxes. Danny asked if their teacher could call the company and tell them. It was at that point that Roberta told the children they could tell the company themselves. The children all thought that was a good idea.

Over the course of the next few days, during writing time, Roberta had the children write rough drafts of what they wanted the crayon/marker company to know about the problem they were having. They talked about what was important information for the manufacturer to know. They also decided to draw pictures to go with their letters. The children conferenced with each other, gave each other feedback, and re-copied their final drafts to make a good copy for sending. Roberta also wrote her own letter to the company, which she shared with her students as a series of mini-lessons, showing them how she planned to organize her comments, talking aloud about tone, and showing how she proofread and corrected her errors.

The package of letters was sent to the company. The actual activity was valuable in and of itself; however, when the children received a response from the company, it added an extra dimension. The children learned the power of their words and how, as consumers, they could voice their opinion and sometimes get a result. It was a model they applied to other items they bought, such as individual milk cartons (they had difficulty opening them) and skipping ropes the school had bought for recess (the handles came off). In all these cases, they received a response from the manufacturer; in the case of the skipping ropes, they were given a new set.

Consider This

As you reflect on this scenario, think about how these five-year-old students learned about the power of language to work through and solve problems. Consider all the opportunities for literacy instruction— reading, viewing and representing, speaking and listening, and writing— that the teacher used to engage and instruct her students.

Toy-Making Report

Toy: _____

Why did you decide to build this toy?

_____

_____

Materials:

Steps in making the toy:

Diagram your process.

What problems did you encounter and how did you deal with them?

Toy Advertising Survey

Hey there! Do you watch Saturday-morning TV? Do you watch all those great toy ads? If you do, please use this form to help you record what you see.

1st: Choose one ad to keep watching. They will probably repeat it several times.

Name the toy: _____

What company makes the toy? _____

2nd: Quickly jot down what happens in the ad.

Describe the setting (where it happens)

_____

_____

Characters : Who (girls/boys), how many

_____

_____

Action: What do the people or characters do?

What does the toy do?

What do the characters say?

_____

_____

Announcer: Is there a voice talking "over" the ad? If so, what is it saying?

_____

_____

3rd: If an illustration would help you remember details, make it on the back of this page.

Two Stars and A Wish

Presenter: _____

**Two things I really like in your Toy Scrapbook (and why)

* 1) _____

_____

_____

_____

_____

* 2) _____

_____

_____

_____

One wish (suggestion) I have for your scrapbook (and why) _____

_____

_____

_____

Responder:_____ Date: _____

6   Working Towards Social Justice

The Bed Project

Every morning in Anna Chase's Grade 2 classroom, her group of 25 children gather in the Conversation Corner to discuss "important and pressing" matters of the day. One day Celia, usually a very quiet but thoughtful child, stood beside Anna as she waited for the children's attention. Celia whispered something into Anna's ear. "Well, Celia," Anna said in a serious tone, "I think this is definitely an important and pressing matter for the class to consider. Have you spoken to Callie? Is she okay with you bringing this to us?" Celia nodded. "Has Callie asked her mom if it is okay?" Another nod. Then Anna asked, "Would you like to go first this morning?" Celia nodded and Anna called the class to order.

Anna has created a space in her busy classroom schedule for students to bring up and discuss issues and matters that are of importance to them. Sometimes they are about things happening in the news or in their local community, and sometimes they are about their school. But unlike most Show-and-Tell or News sessions, Anna has incorporated a social justice focus. Therefore, there is the expectation that some form of action will come out of the issues the children bring forward. Sometimes that action results in a fact-finding mission; other times it may involve inviting in guest speakers or raising money. In this case, Celia asked her friend Callie if she could share what she has found out with the class to see if they could help solve Callie's problem.

When everyone was quiet, Anna gave Celia the go-ahead. In her very quiet but confident voice Celia began, "How many of you have ever slept on the floor?"

With Anna's help, encouraging, asking questions, and keeping students' growing enthusiasm in check, Celia explained that she wanted to bring a problem to her classmates' attention. She asked how students would feel if they had to sleep on the floor all of the time, and if they thought it would be good for them. A lot of discussion ensued, with the consensus being that it would interfere with a person's sleep to lie on the floor, even if they had layers of blankets or a foam pad to sleep on. Celia then shared that this was the situation her friend Callie was in.

The children listen intently as Celia outlined her idea to find a bed for Callie. She asked her classmates how they might go about finding one, given they didn't have any money to buy one. Anna acted as secretary, writing down the ideas on chart paper. As they came to the end of their scheduled conversation time, Anna suggested a committee be struck to discuss the suggestions and to make recommendations to the class. It was decided that Celia should chair the committee and that Callie also be a member. Three other students volunteered to be members. The Committee was to report back to the class in three days, with recommendations for an action plan. Anna asked the school's guidance counselor if she would act as a facilitator for the meetings, which were to be held at lunch time.

When the committee returned to the Conversation Corner three days later, they brought with them pages of chart paper outlining their recommendation. They talked about how they had been thinking about yard sales, the environment, and reducing/reusing/recycling, and had come up with a plan they felt was both good for Callie and good for the environment. They thought they should see if anyone in the class had a bed they didn't want and would be willing to donate. As their idea was discussed, concerns were raised: that the bed needed to be a good one and that they needed a backup plan in case no one in the class had a bed to spare. They also realized they would need help to move a bed, and that they probably had to get permission from the principal before going any further.

Once again, Anna recorded their discussion and drew up a list of actions in response to their concerns/questions. With her help, the class decided on what work needed to be done, and divided the class into the appropriate committees. It was decided that the original committee should go see the principal. Once the principal gave her okay, the other committees began their work—researching types of mattresses and beds, interviewing Callie and her mom to see what kind of bed they had in mind, and drafting a notice to go home to students' parents explaining what they were looking for.

Other groups began their work as the project progressed. It was decided a that committee would view the beds to see if they were suitable. This involved measuring the bed and examining the mattress and other parts to see that they were in good order. In order for the committee to leave school grounds, they also had to arrange for permission and line up transportation, in keeping with school board policy. They had to telephone the donors to schedule the viewing. Once a decision was reached, arrangements had to be made to transport the bed and to set it up in Callie's house.

The entire process was undertaken in a serious and purposeful manner. It was important to Anna that the children be respectful of Callie's and her mom's wishes throughout, and so Anna steered the children towards consulting with them whenever there was a question about how to proceed.

Needless to say, the entire process took a while from start to finish but, after approximately one month, Callie had a bed to sleep in. The class had also managed to get appropriate bedding and an assortment of stuffed animals and bedtime reading—all prerequisites for a good night's sleep.

Spin-offs of the original project resulted in the class becoming actively engaged in researching and participating in global projects, in which they raised funds for children in need of bedding, clothing, and school supplies. They wrote letters of thanks to those who helped, including one to the principal for allowing them to do the project in the first place. And they appeared before a staff meeting to make teachers aware of the possibility that other children in the school may be in the same situation as Callie, and to show that they were willing to share their expertise should it be needed.

The students put what they had learned in their project work to good use as they prepared for the presentation. Prior to the staff meeting, the children once again met in their committees to decide on the information they wanted to convey and how they wanted to share it. They included testimonials from classmates and their teacher about how they felt doing this kind of work, why it was important, and what they learned.

Whether you call them strategies, learning outcomes, or learning objectives, projects such as this also dovetail well with most provincial/state curriculum documents.

This was an authentic literacy project that involved students in multiple aspects of literacy in critical and purposeful ways. A closer look at what these students undertook, along with their teacher, reveals the richness and depth of the literacy engagements provided.

Using the Atlantic Canada English Language Arts Guide as an example, below is a list of related specific curriculum outcomes met.

Specific Curriculum Outcomes	Expectations Students will be expected to…	Learning Experiences Students demonstrated these outcomes when…
Students will speak and listen to explore, extend, clarify, and reflect on their thoughts, ideas, feelings, and experiences.	1. describe, share and discuss their own ideas and those of others 2. present an argument with supporting information 3. ask and respond to questions to clarify information 4. express and explain opinions 5. listen critically to others' ideas 6. problem solve	• bringing up and discussing topics during Conversation Corner and committee work • making the case when seeking permission to undertake the project • arranging for beds to view, organizing transportation, finding out school policies and rules • making the presentation at the staff meeting • deciding what course of action to take on behalf of Callie • gathering information and then choosing an action that best suited the situation
Students will be able to communicate information and ideas effectively and clearly, and respond personally and critically.	1. give and follow instructions, both oral and written 2. adapt volume, projection, facial expression, gestures, and tone of voice to the situation/task	• creating directions to the homes offering beds for drivers • making oral presentations and phone calls, and discussing their opinion or ideas
Students will be able to interact with sensitivity and respect, considering the situation, audience, and purpose.	1. develop an awareness of how language is used appropriately in different situations 2. when to use particular forms of communication (i.e. letter writing, e-mail, in-person, etc.).	• learning from various resource persons and mini-demonstrations by the teacher about the style elements of various forms of communication • deciding to use e-mail, personal contact, or letter writing

Specific Curriculum Outcomes	Expectations Students will be expected to…	Learning Experiences Students demonstrated these outcomes when…
Students will be expected to select, read, and view with understanding a range of literature, information, media, and visual texts.	1. read widely from a variety of sources	• checking the Internet, catalogues, and non-fiction texts regarding the specifications for various beds and mattresses
	2. use the various features of written texts to determine content, locate topics, and obtain information	• seeking information about projects that support children in Canada and other countries
	3. use a variety of self-correcting strategies; word solve; use contextual clues	• reading pamphlets and advertising information in print and on the Internet • gathering information for committee work. • reading e-mail communications and letters
	4. make connections among texts	• comparing information about the beds they were offered with the information they obtained from other sources
	5. organize information orally and in written form	• preparing to make phone calls and write letters to explain the project they were undertaking
Students will be expected to use writing and other forms of representation to explore, clarify, and reflect on the thoughts, feelings, experiences, and learnings, and to use their imagination.	make their own notes	• listening to speakers or reading information.
Students will be expected to create texts collaboratively and independently, using a variety of forms for a range of audiences and purposes.	1. create written texts in a variety of forms 2. consider the reader's/listener's/viewer's questions	• writing letters to donors, making posters, writing e-mails and thank-you notes • responding to questions orally and revising responses in light of these questions
Students will be expected to use a range of strategies to develop effective writing and media products to enhance their clarity, precision, and effectiveness.	1. use a range of pre-writing, drafting, revising, editing, proofreading, and presentation strategies 2. use some conventions of written language (e.g., punctuation and capitalization, language structure, spelling)	• crafting communication about the project to parents, service groups, the principal, and other students, and staff • writing for themselves or others.

Addressing Standards

Although the Bed Project can be seen to address several of the NCTE/IRA Standards (see page 21), the standard this project most exemplifies is

4. Students adjust their use of spoken, written, and visual language (e.g., conventions, style, vocabulary) to communicate effectively with a variety of audiences and for different purposes.

Most importantly, while strengthening literacy skills in use, students also saw the relationship of the skills they were learning and using to the everyday, and the power they had when they used their skills effectively.

Supporting Literacy Learning

In order to help students express their ideas effectively, Anna used the mini-lesson teaching technique to focus students learning on specific skills or strategies they needed to be more effective language users throughout this project. Some mini-lessons were short (a mere five minutes), while others took longer (15 to 20 minutes). Some were aimed at the whole class, while others were designed for small groups or individuals. Each lesson made explicit the role—Code Breaker, Meaning Maker, Text User, Text Analyst—the students were expected to take as they engaged with a variety of texts.

The following list, which relates back to NCTE/IRA English Language Arts Standard #4 and the Atlantic Provinces English Language Arts Curriculum Outcomes listed on pages 79–80, is by no means exhaustive. The teacher

- demonstrated the importance of organization, voice, and standard spelling and grammar in written texts, by using samples from the notices, letters, and reports the student committees were working on
- brought in lots of real-world examples—advertisements, business letters, and minutes of meetings—so that students could deconstruct their content and structure
- showed students how to use the technology available—to send e-mail and search the Internet for online furniture catalogues, information on healthy sleep, and global friendship projects
- demonstrated the advantages and disadvantages of specific modes of communication, and discussed which was most appropriate for the desired outcome—when to send an e-mail, when to go in person
- developed role plays in which students practised making phone calls, speaking to the principal, and answering questions at the staff meeting. Some were audio- and videotaped for feedback.
- invited resource people— the school secretary, a telemarketer, a car salesperson—to demonstrate their skills
- used the think-aloud to question her own reading or writing and to problem-solve how to improve them
- modeled note-taking, agenda-writing, and information storage and retrieval techniques

Through each mini-lesson, the teacher mobilized students' prior knowledge, extending that knowledge by introducing and developing additional skills and strategies.

Although each mini-lesson was led or initiated by the teacher, it was interactive and responsive to the needs of the students.

Instructional Focus: Oral Language Skills

Throughout the project it was necessary for students to use oral language skills to communicate with their peers and adults. Anna demonstrated skills associated with the listening and speaking situations in which the students would be engaged. She used a variety of strategies to help her students understand and practise the skills they would later use.

Making Explicit the Behaviors Required

The teacher brainstormed with the class what various behaviors looked like and then what they sounded like. For instance, they looked at talking to someone on the phone:

1. They brainstormed what this might *look* like while the teacher recorded their responses on chart paper: e.g., listening carefully, making notes.
2. They brainstormed what this would *sound* like: e.g., friendly tone of voice, volume is loud enough to be heard, conversation stays on topic, responds appropriately to what speaker is saying without interrupting.
3. This was followed up by pairing students to practise placing a call and receiving a call about some aspect of the project.

Talking to the Wall

Sometimes students followed Talking to the Wall by joining with a partner and receiving feedback.

In order to build confidence and to help students rehearse what they wanted to say, Anna would have her students spread out around the room with their speech or notes and "talk to the wall." In a soft voice, students practised what they wanted to say.

Questioning

Using a variety of samples of short interviews from magazines and newspapers, the teacher engaged the children in a discussion about what they noticed concerning the interview format: who was speaking, what type of speech the interviewer used, what kind of information was contained in an interview, and who might use the interview or be interested in the interview. She put a portion of the interview on an overhead and they located all the questions that were asked. Next, they brainstormed what they might want to know when questioning those who had beds they were willing to donate. They made a list in the form of statements, and then together rewrote the statements as questions. They also discussed how an interview or conversation flows usually in a logical order and numbered their questions so they were in an appropriate sequence.

Active Listening

An important skill the teacher wanted her students to develop was the ability to listen carefully to what others were saying and to respond appropriately. She used a Fishbowl technique to demonstrate to students what active listening looked like and sounded like:

The Fishbowl technique helps students see and hear what a skill or strategy is like when it is being used, and focuses their attention on specific aspects of that skill.

Listening and speaking skills, just like reading and writing, need demonstration and repeated practice.

1. She sought a student volunteer to talk with her prior to the session. Together they decided on a topic they would talk about and rehearsed a bit of what the students might say—in this case about a camping trip.
2. During the Fishbowl, the teacher and volunteer sat on chairs in the centre of a circle made by the rest of the class. The class had clipboards, pencils, and a record sheet divided into two columns with the headings *Doing/Saying* printed at the top.
3. The watchers were instructed to write in point form what they noticed the teacher doing in the first column and what they heard her saying in the second.
4. The Fishbowl lasts about fifteen minutes and is followed by a debriefing, during which the students share their observations.

Meeting the Needs of Diverse Learners

By offering in a supportive and structured way lots of opportunities to practise, the project helped struggling language learners organize their thoughts, rehearse what they wanted to say, receive positive and supportive feedback, and take an active and meaningful role.

The teacher was careful to make sure that, in group situations, one member of the group did not dominate the group or become the group spokesperson. She used a technique based on Daniels' (2002) roles for students during Literature Circles; this worked especially well during committee meetings and for small-group tasks. Each member of the group took on a specific role:

Questioner: the person who helped the group generate questions
Recorder: the person who took notes
Photographer: the person who recorded notes or other artifacts through digital photography
Fact Finder: the person who brought forward new information
Facilitator: the person who began the meeting and kept it moving
Action Activator: the person who kept track of what needed to be done following the meeting and by whom

Having a role helps struggling students maintain their interest while extending their learning in purposeful and meaningful ways.

These roles rotated, allowing all students the opportunity to develop the different skills.

Assessing for Student Growth

An important aspect of using classroom assessment practices to support student learning is ensuring that all students know what successful learning looks like. During this project, the teacher had many opportunities to help her students have a clear vision of the expected learning. Together they developed criteria for the various tasks, and students were encouraged to use those criteria throughout the process to measure their own growth and focus their learning. Early in the process students, discussed "what would make a good bed." The teacher made a list of the factors to be considered and all the tasks to be completed in order to achieve their goal. This list helped students stay focused and keep the end in sight, and let them know when they were making successful progress towards their goal. When they finished, the list became a support (reference) for reflecting and responding to the process.

Other discussions and clearly laid-out lists or charts—such as "What makes a good thank-you letter?" and "What would make a good presentation to the staff?"—helped students consider what success would look like in those situations, and what their various audiences might need/want from their communication attempts. Making those factors clear for all students in advance of doing the work increases their confidence in what is expected and produces fewer hit-and-miss results.

Involving Parents and Community

The teacher employed some important strategies when involving parents and community members in this project:

1. She set the tone from the start. She conveyed respect for the family and their interests by consulting them and seeking their input and permission before beginning.
2. She drew upon the knowledge and expertise of the community to help with demonstrations of the skills the students were learning to use.
3. She used parent volunteers—as furniture movers, drivers, potential donors, etc.—to enact the children's plans.
4. She helped her students articulate what they were learning.

The Town Hall Meeting

This project began when a group of Grade 6 students came to speak with the principal about a matter that concerned them. The school had just been inducted into the League of Peaceful Schools and this group of students was disturbed by the growing use of Magik™ Cards—a card-based role-playing game popular with students in Grades 5 to 7. In their opinion, the cards depicted violence and should be banned from use in school.

Unfamiliar with the cards, the principal decided to seek out students playing with them to see what they had to say. After speaking with the game enthusiasts, it was clear that there were differences of opinion about the cards. On one side, students wanting the cards banned felt that playing with the images and roles led to violence, while those on the other side felt that, as long as students did not engage in violent behavior, the card game should be permitted. In addition, there was a much broader issue that had implications for future school activities—what it meant to be a peaceful school.

The principal took the matter to the staff, who were themselves divided. After considerable discussion, the principal proposed a school-wide project that she hoped would resolve the matter to everyone's satisfaction. It was decided that the school would hold a referendum on Magik™ Cards. Prior to the vote, there would be a Town Hall meeting, during which the issues would be presented and debated.

In their classrooms, students were organized into committees and discussion groups. Some researched referendums—their purpose, how they are run, when they are used, how the vote is conducted, who is eligible to vote. It was this committee's task to design how the school referendum would be conducted and to present that information to the voters.

Other groups researched democracy and the right to vote. Still others looked into Magik™ Cards themselves: How did they get started? Who makes them? Were there any other issues or concerns raised on the Internet regarding their use? Yet another group contacted the founder of the League of Peaceful Schools, to solicit her opinion on what constituted appropriate behavior for a peaceful school and to seek permission to contact other member schools for their opinions. A group of Grade 5 students wanted to find out just how much Magik™ Card playing was going on at the school. With the help of a marketing expert, they constructed a survey to be given to students. This brought up issues of ethics and consent, and whether participation in the survey and in the voting should be mandatory; a local university researcher spoke with them on these issues.

Eventually it was decided that the legal age to vote would be ten and up, and that voters had to be registered at the school. A date was decided upon for the vote, and polling stations were created, voter rosters assembled, officials assigned to the various roles, and provision made for announcing the results on the public address system and in the school newsletter.

One Grade 7 class wanted to put out a special issue of the school newsletter. They worked with a local reporter to write articles that gave the background of the issue, discussed the controversy, announced the date of the referendum, and invited the community to a Town Hall meeting at which the issues would be debated. They also solicited letters to the editor.

Another class took charge of the Town Hall. They researched rules of deportment and distributed them to the classes eligible to participate. They brainstormed moderators and agreed upon the person they felt best fit their criteria to be chair of the local Village Commission. They met with the moderator and discussed how the room would be organized, the time limits given for arguments and rebuttals, and how to handle questions or comments from the floor. Participating classes chose representatives to present the positive and negative side of the argument. The representatives of each class met with an adult facilitator to plan their presentation and to rehearse its delivery.

The Town Hall meeting took place during the week, early in the evening so younger children could attend. The gym was filled with parents, community members, and students from other grade levels. Both sides of the issue were argued and questions from the floor were answered. The Referendum Committee closed the meeting by reviewing the voter regulations, announcing the date of the vote, and clarifying the locations of the polling booths on both floors of the school.

The vote was held one week later. By a close margin, the voters decided Magik™ Cards would stay. The results were announced throughout the school, in the school newsletter, and even on the local public-television station. As part of their argument, those in favor of allowing Magik™ Cards had put forth a set of responsibilities for those engaging in Magik™ Card play. Following the decision, that group created posters reminding players and others of their responsibilities and hung them throughout the school.

Consider This

1. How were outcomes, learning objectives, or standards addressed?
2. What teaching strategies were used to support students' literacy learning?
3. How might classroom assessment practices support student growth?
4. How were parents and community involved?

7   Connecting Literacy across the Curriculum

Watershed Conference

As part of a middle-school science class, Pat Carson shared with his class the definition of a watershed as being any area within 50 km of an ocean. In response, one student commented that, given the definition, the entire province of Nova Scotia was a watershed. As the students discussed how water was an integral part of every Nova Scotian's life, many scientific and social issues came to the fore. The students decided to extend their discussion and ask their families about the part water played in their personal and professional lives. They examined newspapers and magazines, noting how water was often a factor in many local, national, and global issues: the decline of the lobster fishery, harbor clean-up, the ownership of the beaches, the royalties from off-shore exploration, the pollution from the run-offs of farms and golf courses, tourism, drug smuggling, etc.

In this small junior high there was a yearly science fair where students were required to put together science displays to present to teachers and parents. Year after year, students and their parents strove to find something new and spectacular. The displays always covered a wide range of science-based topics. Some students, often from homes in which at least one family member was involved in some aspect of science or technology in their professional lives, would produce amazing displays with the support of their families. Other students went online and found a science-fair topic to recreate. The results were varied in quality and interest. The Grade 8 science teacher found that science-fair preparation took a large amount of time and energy, and yet seemed to result in little understanding of how science was part of the students' world.

Given the growing interest and enthusiasm for the topic of "water," Pat talked to the students about scientific conferences where groups of scientists and researchers get together to examine various aspects of a particular issue. He suggested they might participate in a scientific conference rather than the traditional science fair. They would title their conference *Nova Scotia: the Watershed Province*. The students were enthusiastic. After conferring with his grade-level colleagues, Pat announced that participation in the conference would take the place of all or part of the end-of-year exams in science, social studies, English language arts, and mathematics. In keeping with the conference format, students could choose to present a paper on scientific or social issues related to science, run a workshop, or develop a display or demonstration related to the topic. In addition, after the conference, students would submit an assessment package and go through an individual interview. Each student was given a detailed written outline of the expectations for the project and a second copy was sent home so that parents would be informed.

Students were to work in groups of three. Once groups were formed, their first task was to discuss procedures for making group decisions and for getting work accomplished. Since this was a multi-disciplinary project, students would need to use their materials in different classes, so each student kept a work folder for materials and learning logs to track their daily progress. In addition, each student was asked to keep a Water Log, a personal learning journal that included what they were learning, what new questions or ideas they had, what was working or not working in their group. Throughout the project, their teachers would monitor the journals and give written feedback, directing or focusing the student's efforts.

During their English classes, the students learned about the three possible types of presentations—a scientific or social paper, a workshop, or a display/demonstration. Students were encouraged to think about which of the various presentation methods would best suit their topic. In addition, the students talked about writing proposals and what information the committee members would need to have in order to approve their request. At one point, a question about the biases and personal preferences of committee members led to a discussion on the value of a committee approach, which resulted in roles and cautions for committee members. In science classes, students explored the topic of water systems on the earth, particularly as they had impact on their province. In social studies classes, the teacher focused on having students explore how past events influenced the present, especially around issues related to government policy and practice. In math class, students worked with data—finding ways to create it, analyze it, and use it in their presentations.

After each group of three had decided on a specific topic, they wrote a proposal outlining their topic, posing some guiding questions, listing possible sources of information, and choosing a presentation method. The proposal was submitted to a committee of teachers and students for review, who read and discussed each one, provided the group with feedback and suggestions, and made sure that there was an overall balance of topics and methods for the whole conference.

In addition to traditional print and media sources, all students were encouraged to use primary sources in their community. Since a major university with a large science department was within walking distance of the school, many students contacted scientists, researchers, and technicians involved in interesting and related projects. Others contacted local experts, businesses, and politicians by telephone, through e-mail, and in person. Many of these local sources were later invited to attend and evaluate the conference.

Especially during the latter weeks of the project, students were given class time to work on their conference presentations. This allowed teachers to circulate among the groups and to meet with groups or individuals as needed. In addition, a number of parent volunteers were invited to support and supervise the groups as they worked all over the school building—the library, the computer stations, the art room, the technical education lab, and the hallways—anywhere they could find space and resources.

Meanwhile, a Grade 9 community service class and their teacher took on the task of managing the conference logistics. The Grade 9 students interviewed professional conference arrangers about the process, then made work plans, developed a conference package, determined location and timetable schedules, consulted with staff, located and arranged for spaces and audio-visual requirements, kept a budget, called special guests, and submitted a final report with costs, highlights, problems, and recommendations for future conferences.

The Grade 7 students were invited to attend the conference and were asked to fill out evaluation forms for the sessions they attended. A group of Grade 8 students took copies of the evaluation forms to the Grade 7 classes several days before the conference. They discussed the purpose and theme of the conference and explained how to use the evaluation forms. As well, a number of scientists and local community members were invited and asked to fill out written evaluation forms. The completed forms, with criteria that had been developed by the students and teachers together, were to be given back to the presenters at the end of each session and included as part of their assessment packages.

Throughout the project, the teachers and students discussed the world of scientific conferences, thinking about who attends them and why, who doesn't and why, how are they useful, what are some of the problems with them. Students interviewing people who attended scientific conferences shared their comments.

The evening before the conference, families of the students were invited to come to a special session where groups and individuals had an opportunity to present their work. The morning of the conference, the whole school was involved. The Grade 9 conference group was ensuring that all was ready, greeting guests and handling last-minute crises. The Grade 8 students were nervously reviewing their materials, and the Grade 7 students were anxious to get started. After a brief welcome and congratulations by the principal, the conference got underway. Students and guests moved through the sessions, the displays, and the workshops smoothly. Students, teachers, scientists, and other community people mingled, talked, and shared the learning experience.

As a multi-disciplinary unit, the Watershed project addressed learning outcomes for many subjects: science, social studies, mathematics, and English language arts. At the beginning of the unit, students were provided with a comprehensive list of learning outcomes in four subjects. The outcomes were discussed in each class and students were asked to consider what they already knew about each. Parents were provided with written copies of the outcomes (see below) along with a detailed description of the project requirements and purpose. The teachers met regularly to develop and coordinate experiences. Using the Nova Scotia Learning Outcomes Framework for Grade 8, the parents and students were provided with the following list.

In **social studies**, students will be expected to

- demonstrate an understanding of the interactions among people, places, and the environment
- acquire, process, and utilize information, applying a variety of thinking skills and strategies, to communicate effectively in social studies
- demonstrate an understanding of the interaction and interdependence of people, science, and technology

In **mathematics**, students will be expected to

- communicate and interpret information obtained from data collected
- construct three graphs: circle, line, bar

- give the mean, median, and mode of data obtained from the research, and indicate which of these three would be most appropriate to use
- interpret information from their graphs

In **science**, in relation to the topic of "water systems of the world" students will explore

- the nature of science and technology
- the relationship between science and technology
- the social and environmental contexts of science and technology

Students will develop the skills of

- initiating and planning
- performing and recording
- analyzing and interpreting
- communication and teamwork

Students will know

- how waves and tides are generated and how they interact with shorelines
- how the process of erosion and deposition results from wave action and water flow
- the interactions of the ocean currents, winds, and regional climates
- how to analyze factors that affect productivity and species distribution in marine and freshwater environments

In English **language arts**, students will be expected to

- communicate information and ideas effectively and clearly, and respond personally and critically
- interact with sensitivity and respect considering the audience and purpose
- interpret, select, and combine information using a variety of strategies, resources, and technologies
- respond critically to a range of texts, applying their understanding of language, form, and genre
- use a range of strategies to develop effective writing and other ways of representing, and to enhance their clarity, precision, and effectiveness

Addressing Standards

Using the broader perspective of the NCTE/IRA English Language Arts Standards (see page 21), this project gave students the opportunity to

7. Participate as knowledgeable, reflective, creative, and critical members of a variety of literacy communities.

Many groups chose very controversial topics to explore, such as the clean up of Halifax Harbour, the decline of the lobster fishery, beach ownership in Nova Scotia. Their teachers stressed the importance of being aware of and sensitive to

During the conference, the invited experts often commented on the depth and breadth of the students' knowledge, and more than one expert had a lively conversation with specific groups.

all perspectives before they chose a position for themselves on the topic. Many found that politicians, businesspeople, environmentalists, scientists, their parents, and the "person on the street" had widely differing opinions. Collecting those opinions and examining the reasons given, through personal contact and various written sources—from scientific journals to newspapers, documentaries to popular TV shows—allowed students to feel confident in their own informed opinions.

Supporting Literacy Learning

Secondary teachers working in all subjects have long been told that everyone is a teacher of literacy. In this project, each teacher took the responsibility to help students learn how language is used within their discipline and across all disciplines.

Instructional Focus: Applying Literacy Strategies across the Curriculum

Since this project was interdisciplinary, the ELA teacher took the opportunity to work with her colleagues to make sure these strategies were part of the work in each discipline.

As part of their English language arts class, most students were familiar and comfortable with using many literacy support strategies, such as brainstorming, graphic organizers, concept webs, K–W–L, QU–I–C (QUestions, Information, Connections), using information from text features. The teachers' goal was to help students understand that learning to use such strategies in one area would help them in other areas.

QU–I–C in Science

Pat introduced the QU–I–C Organizer (see page 98) in science class. On large pieces of chart paper, each group developed a three-column "quick" overview record of their progress. In the first column, they listed Questions (QU) they had at the beginning and added new questions throughout the process. In the second column, they recorded new information (I) about their topic, particularly in regard to their listed questions. In the third column, they recorded connections (C) made between their group topic and the main topic of the conference—how being a watershed influenced the lives of all Nova Scotians. This chart, which was reviewed at the beginning of each working session, was used to help students stay focused and organized. It also allowed Pat to see at a quick glance where the groups were in their progress.

Using Text Features in Math

The math teacher focused on the importance of using certain text features when reading and interpreting information presented in tables, graphs, and charts. Students discovered how careful reading of titles and captions helped them understand the statistical material found in reports, newspaper articles, and magazines.

PREP in Social Studies

Part of the requirements for their assignments included students having an informed opinion on the effects of their specific topic on the lives of Nova Scotians. Students needed to be able to construct and articulate their arguments clearly. To support this, the social studies teacher re-introduced the PREP structure (Wydro, 1981) that the language arts teacher had used previously with the students in writing opinion pieces.

Point of view   ⇒ Clearly state your position.
Reasons why   ⇒ Give reasons and facts.
Evidence or examples   ⇒ Offer concrete examples.
Point of view (restated)   ⇒ Restate your position and include any action you think is appropriate for you or your audience to take.

The social studies teacher helped the students use this structure to not only think through and write out their opinions, but to practise speaking them in a concise, clear way.

The teachers in each of the disciplines helped students to see how language and literacy strategies were important in every aspect of their work.

Subject	Related Literacy Goals Students will be expected to…	Teacher Instruction
Science	1. select and integrate information from various print and electronic sources 2. identify new questions and problems that arise from what is learned 3. communicate questions, ideas, intentions, plans, and results using notes in point form, sentences, data tables, graphs, drawings, oral language, and other means	• promoted the use of numerous sources of information on a topic • provided a wide variety of written science materials, including popular science magazines, government and scientific reports, newspaper articles, website addresses. • demonstrated strategies for reading difficult scientific texts • shared samples of scientists' journals • demonstrated the use of graphic organizers and note-taking matrices • helped students prepare questions to interview scientists and other experts
Social Studies	1. ask complex geographic questions 2. acquire, organize, and analyze geographic information and answer geographic questions 3. analyze selected issues to illustrate the interdependence among people, technology, and the environment	• demonstrated strategies for reading complex social texts • demonstrated the use of graphic organizers and note-taking matrices • encouraged students to seek primary sources of information • encouraged students to look at topics from various perspectives—political, big business, small business, uninformed citizenry, financial, etc.

Subject	Related Literacy Goals Students will be expected to…	Teacher Instruction
Mathematics	1. solve problems involving the collection, display, and analysis of data 2. interpret information from their graphs	• provided students with opportunities to learn and use the language of data and statistics • helped students to learn to read problems carefully
English Language Arts	1. communicate information and ideas effectively and clearly, and to respond personally and critically 2. interact with sensitivity and respect, considering the audience and purpose 3. interpret, select, and combine information using a variety of strategies, resources, and technologies 4. respond critically to a range of texts, applying their understanding of language, form, and genre 5. use a range of strategies to develop effective writing and other ways of representing, and to enhance their clarity, precision, and effectiveness	• provided students with samples of scientific papers to examine and develop criteria • posted student-generated criteria for the various formats and encouraged them to use the guidelines to self-assess throughout the process • helped students to brainstorm questions about their topic before researching • supported students' use of visual supports (diagrams, graphs, charts, labeled drawings, etc.) and organizational supports (indexes, tables of content, glossaries, text boxes, titles, etc.) to read technical texts • worked with groups of students to develop interviewing techniques and ways to write up the information • set up and monitored peer editing groups • met with project groups regularly, going over their proposals, their progress, and any group problems • met with individuals to help them set goals and timelines for themselves, particularly those students with organizational difficulties • encouraged students to role play situations where each group member would take a different perspective on their issue • taught lessons on how to cite reference materials correctly

Meeting the Needs of Diverse Learners

Most students benefited from the support of working with a group. The school resource and learning-centre personnel worked with groups that included students with more challenging learning issues. In several cases, the support personnel helped specific students with very high needs to design projects that were within their interest range and provided enough challenge for their growth in learning. For example, one student who loved tugboats worked on learning how to interview a tugboat captain and how to present the information about the problems in the harbor. He presented his project alongside the group who was studying the pollution problems of Halifax Harbour. For him, his literacy learning was in the form of learning how to formulate questions, making a telephone call to set up an appointment, asking the questions, taking relevant digital photos, and presenting the information on a display board.

Assessing for Student Growth

In a project such as this, with a number of teachers working together, it was very important that students be very clear about the learning targets or outcomes they were expected to address.

Rubrics

Together with their English and science teachers, the students brainstormed what would be important criteria to consider when evaluating a student's participation in the conference. They turned the guidelines into an evaluation rubric (see page 99) for the teachers to use to evaluate the final assessment package. They then chose several important criteria to develop the conference rubric for student evaluators—the physical presentation (or visuals), the oral presentation, ability to communicate data. Under each of these main criteria, they wrote descriptors (evidence) for five levels of achievement. This proved to be a difficult task; it took the groups a long time and much discussion before they could agree. As a result, they decided it was important to meet with the Grade 7 classes in advance so they could explain the rubric before they had to use it.

The adult evaluators (teachers, experts, community, and school board) used a more complex rubric prepared by the teachers, which included relevancy and accuracy of content, and an evaluation of the appropriateness of the presentation method chosen.

Copies of these rubrics were provided for the students and their parents at the beginning of the project, and were posted in the classroom and referred to throughout the project.

Assessment During the Project

In order to evaluate students at the end of such a complex unit of work, the teachers used many sources of assessment information. In addition to observing behavior during class time, the teachers looked at the group proposal, individual notes from the working files, the daily tracking sheets, the personal learning journals or Water Logs, a mid-point interview, the group's bibliographies, the actual conference presentation, and the evaluation sheets from students and expert guests. Teachers used all these sources of assessment information to make constant instructional decisions for both individuals and groups. Oral and written feedback helped students stay focused and on-track. In a project with so many different activities going on at the same time, it was the teachers' concern that some students could "get lost." Having students keep track of their own work, the teachers could monitor the progress quickly and provide additional support for those having problems.

The Water Logs were particularly important since they allowed students keep track of their accomplishments, reflect upon their learning, record ideas, and ask for specific help. The teachers regularly monitored the Logs, and students were encouraged to submit them whenever they had a question that couldn't be answered during class time. At the end of the project, students used their Logs to

As an emphasis for this project was how to collect and use information from primary sources, the teacher and students discussed what kinds of information could be gathered from people. They explored different ways to ask the same question and developed a set of guidelines for being a respectful yet effective interviewer. They prepared a "good interview" checklist so that they could evaluate themselves after each interview.

help write their final written reflection and prepare for their individual interviews.

Final Reflection and Interview

After the conference, students compiled their assessment packages and wrote their final reflections. Several days before the final individual interviews, students were given a copy of the interview evaluation guidelines the teacher teams were going to use. It included questions such as

- Where is the science component of your project, the social studies component, the English and mathematics components?
- Did you notice that people in your group took on specific roles? What were those roles; did they help the group to function smoothly?
- While you were doing your research, what information impressed you most?
- In reference to your topic, are there different points of view with regard to the subject?
- Why is Nova Scotia considered a watershed and what are some of the ways it affects our lives?
- What personal actions could you take to improve the conditions of _____ (your project topic)?

Involving Parents and Community

Students involved their parents early in the process by seeking their input into the discussion about how water affects the lives of all Nova Scotians. Since a research focus was the use of primary sources, students sought information from many other people in the community—from local politicians to university experts and people working in relevant government departments and agencies. Not only was the community asked for input, many guests invited to attend and participate in evaluating the conference. Members of the school advisory council and the school board were invited to attend and participate.

Early in the process, a package including an outline of the project, the expectations, the timelines, and the learning outcomes that would be addressed—as well as a copy of the working rubric—was sent home for the parents to review, sign, and return. In such a complex undertaking, it was important to keep parents well-informed. Parents with jobs or interests that were relevant to the topic were invited to come into class and share with all the students. A special session of the conference was held so that any parents or family who could not attend during the day could attend the evening before.

The Science Magazine

Dorothy Winton, a Grade 9 science teacher, wanted to have her students review what they had learned in their science classes throughout the year, and for them to think about how science was part of each of their lives. For years, she had prepared year-end formal exams with questions for each of the science topics they had covered as part of the mandated curriculum. She had a file folder of old tests and exams to choose questions from—but so did the students. Copies of her old exams were passed around by the students from previous years. The most conscientious students would go over the past exams, write out the questions, and memorize answers. Other students read them over and studied those sections of their notes. Still others just froze at the thought of writing any exams. And Dorothy waned at the thought of reading the same information over and over.

Dorothy had noticed that her students loved to read magazines—teen magazines, fashion magazines, auto and motorcycle magazines, sports and daredevil magazines. Instead of a traditional end-of-year examination, she decided to combine the students' interest in and knowledge of the magazine genre with the science topics they had covered. So she suggested that the students each write a science magazine instead of a traditional exam. The magazine would focus on the science topics and concepts for the year: space exploration, reproduction, electricity, and atoms and elements.

Dorothy and the students began by brainstorming what they knew about magazines as a genre—the formats, the parts, the ways in which information was presented, etc. She then provided them with copies of published science-oriented magazines from *National Geographic* to the *Smithsonian* to *OWL*. In pairs, the students studied the magazines and added to their brainstorms. They looked at how similar information about a topic can be presented in many ways within the same magazine—a feature article, did-you-know boxes, a photographic essay, a letter to the editor, a timeline, an opinion piece, even a crossword or logic puzzle. With the help of the art teacher, they studied the basics of page layout and the design elements of space, color, and lettering.

Dorothy gave the students parameters for their magazine. It was to be written for a teen audience and had to include information on all four of the science topics, with a full-length feature article on each of at least two of the topics. She gave the students an outline of the topics and subtopics they had studied during the year.

Dorothy had the students read a number of the feature articles from the science magazines she had collected, and discuss in groups specific examples of what they found interesting and how the authors made their message either clear or confusing. They looked at how authors made complex ideas accessible to readers by the use of charts, graphs, everyday examples, glossaries, etc. Dorothy challenged her students to find ways to make some of the scientific concepts they had studied both interesting and understandable for other teen readers.

Students had three weeks to work on their magazines. Dorothy met with groups of students regularly to share and give feedback on their progress. Students shared their ideas. Dorothy had developed a rubric to evaluate the magazines and she provided the students with a copy to use while they worked.

At the end of three weeks, the students shared their magazines with one another, then handed them in to the teacher. Dorothy asked her students for feedback on the assignment. Most students had enjoyed the challenge of writing a science magazine, had found it an interesting way to review the year's work, and had fun putting the assignment together. Other students, generally those who did well on tests, complained that writing a magazine was much more work than studying for an exam.

Using her rubric, Dorothy evaluated each magazine and returned them to the students with her written comments as well as their numerical grade. As she passed them back, Dorothy took the time to point out something special in each magazine.

While the evaluation of the work took as much time as marking exams, Dorothy was delighted with the overall results. Many students had found interesting ways to present information and many had taken interesting perspectives from which to write.

Consider This

1. How did Dorothy incorporate student interests and knowledge of pop culture into classroom assessment?
2. What must a teacher consider when undertaking such projects?
3. What similar opportunities might you have in your classroom?

QU–I–C Organizer

QUestions	Information	Connections

Grade 8 Watershed Conference Rubric

Presenting group: _____   Evaluator's name: _____

	1	2	3	4	5
Oral Presentation	Confused, ill-prepared; can't hear the voice; speaker seems distracted; poor posture; reads script word-by-word	Little eye contact; voice too low or too high; reads mostly from the script; lacks energy	Reasonable amount of eye contact; some energy; reasonably confident; refers regularly to notes to stay organized	Good eye contact; energetic and confident; refers occasionally to notes; appears well-prepared and organized	Great eye contact and posture; refers only rarely to notes; appears very confident and passionate about topic; presentation appears to be rehearsed
Ability to Communicate	Cannot answer any questions; answers not understandable; able to recall few or no relevant facts	Answers few questions; answers are very brief with little information; uses a few facts to answer questions	Some knowledge of relevant facts; able to answer some questions; some confusion on other questions; most answers understandable	Answers most questions; answers are understandable; good knowledge of facts	Answers questions easily and with detail; seems confident answering questions; explanations are clear and easy to understand; extremely knowledgeable about the topic
Visuals	Lack of care shown in arranging and attaching visuals; few visuals used; visuals used do not appear to connect clearly to the topic	Some attention to placement of visuals but still large empty spaces or crowded sections; lack of color or impact in visuals used; messy lettering in titles and captions	Visuals are interesting and organized; visuals provide some impact; reasonable use of color and space	Visuals are eye-catching and colorful; overall display(s) well-organized; attracts audience and supports the topic	Extremely eye-catching; visuals add another dimension to the topic of the presentation; display engages the audience; out-of-the-ordinary

Mary Lou Peterson and Joe Morrison. Reproduced with permission.

8 Making Connections between Life and Literature

Adolescent Fictions and Non-fictions

Todd Wells was just about at the end of his rope with his Grade 12 English class. Headed either for the work force or to vocation-related postsecondary education, the students openly expressed their dislike for literature—especially poetry!—and resisted all his attempts to engage them. Fortunately, he had been able to develop positive relationships with the students through his efforts to initiate activities that they would find interesting and worthwhile. Still, he was not achieving what he would have liked with the group, lamenting to colleagues that this might be the last opportunity to convince these students that literature offered something to them.

One day early in October, a group of four or five students came into the classroom, deep in animated conversation. As he greeted them, Todd asked, "What's going on?" One of the students waved a newspaper headline in his face, urging, "Just look at this!" The headline on a front-page article about a recent wave of swarmings and thefts attributed to young people in the community screamed, *"What's Wrong with Today's Teens?"* After scanning the paper and settling the students, Todd asked, "So what's the problem?" In outrage, Sarah, one of the most agitated students, repeated, "What's the problem?! Can't you see? It makes it sound like all teens are out every night attacking and robbing people. Most of us have never committed a crime or even gotten in trouble in school." The discussion that ensued was one of the liveliest Todd had experienced with the class. Everyone offered examples of limiting and inaccurate portrayals of teens—on television shows, in movies, in the news, in ads, through music, and in adult conversations.

Over the next few days, as he reflected on what had happened in class, Todd decided to build on the teachable moment created by the students' discussion of the news article. He began to brainstorm ideas for developing an inquiry into images of adolescents in texts, and asked the students for their reaction the next time the class met. The students were more than eager to drop their unit on short stories and pick up on Todd's alternative plan. He shared his beginning brainstorm of ideas and invited them to add their suggestions. Accepting and recording all the suggestions, Todd guided the students towards an opening activity, in which they collected as many examples as they could find of texts with images of adolescents. Prior to the class, Todd had compiled a number of different examples of different types of texts—oral, print, visual, and multimedia—to show the students the scope of what they should be including in their searches. At this point in the investigation, the focus was primarily on media (magazine and newspaper articles, ads in print and electronic forms, television shows, movies, and music) because those were the texts with which students most frequently engaged outside of school.

Over the next week or two, the students collected and examined many different texts, discussing the variety of images of adolescents they discovered. Todd wove in lessons that focused students on *how* the texts created the images through words and visuals, expanding students' critical awareness and insights into how texts work. When the class had compiled quite a large collection, Todd guided them through a process of categorizing the examples. Students enjoyed coming up with names for the categories—Adolescent as Thug, Adolescent as Airhead, Adolescent as Sex Kitten, etc. As they worked with the categorization and critical analysis, the students began to raise questions about contrasting images based on gender, race, culture, and social class: for example, most of the thugs were working-class males, less often Caucasian than other races; most of the airheads were Caucasian females, frequently blonde. The students began by organizing the information on a matrix posted in the classroom. As the compilation of the data became more complex and cumbersome, a group of students took responsibility for creating an electronic database.

After Todd observed the students' engagement in this initial text survey, it was clear to him that the students remained keenly interested in the topic. In fact, as it turned out, the inquiry continued through the entire semester and culminated with a public display of the students' work. The students themselves came up with the idea of going public a few weeks into their study, asserting that it would be an ideal way to paint a more complex picture of who adolescents *really* are. Once they had explored images in contemporary media texts, the students responded positively to Todd's invitation to explore the portrayal of adolescents in literature. With the assistance of the school librarian, he created a diverse collection of fiction related to adolescents. The texts included traditional and graphic novels and short fiction, depicting contemporary adolescents from a variety of cultures, as well as texts written and/or set in the past. He chose one book to read aloud to the students, and incorporated discussions and strategy lessons related to reading fiction as part of the group sharing of the text. Students engaged in independent and small-group reading and discussions. Where there were multiple copies of texts available, students formed literature circles.

The students' reading and discussion of fictional texts expanded the inquiry, leading students to consider the similarities and differences in images across the many different kinds of texts that they had read. They talked about the complex relationships among fiction and non-fiction texts produced in a particular time and place, coming to understand that all texts have impact on and are influenced by the social, historical, political, and cultural contexts in which they are created. They examined how images of adolescents in fiction change over time and across cultures. They raised questions about stereotypes based on gender, race, culture, and social class. They debated whether there is such a thing as a "boy's book" or a "girl's book." The students examined ads and book covers for adolescent fiction and discussed how they help to reproduce or challenge stereotypes. The discussions led to individual and small-group inquiries that took students in a variety of directions. Projects included

- writing and producing pilots for TV shows that depicted adolescents realistically

- creating individual websites highlighting positive accomplishments of members of the class
- designing ads with appeal to real rather than stereotypical teens
- writing stories and plays about adolescents from an adolescent perspective
- studying how adolescents and adolescence has changed through history
- viewing movies and television shows from different decades to compare and contrast images of adolescents
- interviewing parents and grandparents about when they were adolescents, and examining family photos and other memorabilia to add to the picture of teens in other eras
- creating collages: contrasting images of teens today, teens in different eras, images of males and females, etc.
- writing song lyrics reflecting adolescent perspectives, putting songs to music and performing
- adding to the ever-expanding corpus of texts

—until Todd had to say, "Stop!"

At the conclusion of the inquiry the students mounted a two-day-and-evening exhibition of their work in the school gymnasium. They called it *Adolescents on Adolescence*, and invited parents, community members, the media, and school-board officials to attend. The class chose students to be media spokespersons, and designed a press release and press kit. They were disappointed that the electronic media did not cover the event, but were happy with the article that appeared in the feature section of the local paper the following weekend. In their final reflections on the project, students expressed frustration with how hard it is to get media attention for positive accomplishments, but satisfaction with the effort they had collectively made to tell a more complex story about adolescents and adolescence.

Most curricular frameworks for English language arts include an emphasis on students exploring a wide range of texts. The province of Alberta, for example, has established minimum requirements for text study and creation. Had Todd been a teacher in Alberta, his students would more than have met the minimum requirements through their extended inquiry.

In the final year of high school, Alberta students like those in Todd's class are required to study either a novel or book-length non-fiction; a feature film; a modern or Shakespearean play; a variety of poetry (including song) and short stories; visual and multimedia texts; an essay; and popular non-fiction (news stories, feature articles, interviews, and other forms of informative text). Each student must create personal responses and critical/analytical responses to a variety of texts in a range of print and non-print forms.

The types of learning experiences that evolved in Todd's classroom created possibilities for students who had been disengaged from school literacy to accomplish the outcomes for the Grade 12 curriculum as stated in the Alberta Education Program Outline (2003). The students' purposeful and varied use of reading, writing, speaking, listening, viewing, and representing, as they investigated a topic about which they cared passionately, resulted in meaningful learning that also addressed external expectations such as the following:

1. Students will listen, speak, read, write, view, and represent to explore thoughts, ideas, feelings, and experiences.

2. Students will listen, speak, read, write, view, and represent to comprehend literature and other texts in oral, print, visual, and multimedia forms, and respond personally, critically, and creatively.
3. Students will listen, speak, read, write, view, and represent to manage ideas and information.
4. Students will listen, speak, read, write, view, and represent to create oral, print, visual, and multimedia texts, and enhance the clarity and artistry of communication.
5. Students will listen, speak, read, write, view, and represent to respect, support, and collaborate with others.

Addressing Standards

Although the investigation that unfolded in Todd's classroom did not start out as a study of literature, he was able to take advantage of the students' interests to engage them in an aspect of the language-arts curriculum that they previously had resisted. Through his purposeful extension of their student-initiated inquiry, this teacher created a learning context that very powerfully and effectively addressed a broad range of curricular expectations. The learning encompassed all of the NCTE/IRA Standards (see page 21) and provided a particular focus on

2. Students read a wide range of literature from many periods in many genres to build an understanding of the many dimensions (e.g. philosophical, ethical, aesthetic) of human experience.

The students' exploration of images of adolescents across contemporary and historical literature helped them gain insights into their own experiences, and more broadly into the ways in which cultural, social, and historical contexts affect people's lives. Once the students became engaged in reading and thinking about these issues in relation to adolescents in literature, there was a much greater likelihood of enticing them to move their reading beyond the familiar world of adolescence.

Supporting Literacy Learning

Many of the students in Todd's class had not experienced success with literacy learning throughout the earlier grades. While they were eager to participate in the inquiry into images of adolescents, the majority of them needed support in order to be successful learners and participants. As well, Todd's goal was to extend all students' learning as much as possible through appropriate instruction. Although students' individual learning needs varied across the many different contexts in which they learned, Todd designed instruction for a number of broad purposes.

Instructional Purpose	The Teacher...
To generate and sustain students' motivation and confidence as literacy learners	• invited students' active engagement in planning learning experiences and accepted their suggestions • gave students positive feedback on their contributions • interacted frequently with students individually to highlight strengths and accomplishments and to provide necessary guidance
To help students gain access to a range of texts	• provided access to a variety of texts with differing levels of complexity in ideas, form, and language • demonstrated reading strategies and personal and critical response when reading aloud • engaged students in small-group shared reading, with a guiding framework for discussion • highlighted reading strategies in mini-lessons
To enhance students' engagement with literature and their knowledge of literary genres and features of literary texts	• showed students how texts work through examining how different authors handle elements of fiction (setting, plot, character, theme, point of view, style, and language) • encouraged students to draw upon their knowledge of media texts (movies, TV shows) to understand how literary texts work • used song to help students understand poetry • taught students to use graphic organizers, such as character webs, story maps, and chapter grids
To improve students' ability to organize and manage information	• taught students how to construct and name categories to organize information and ideas • drew on students' expertise to incorporate databases and spreadsheets as organizing tools
To teach students inquiry processes	• helped students divide large projects into a logical sequence of tasks and keep track of progress • taught lessons on specific facets of inquiry: developing good inquiry question(s), planning, sources of information, making notes, choosing a form in which to share information, etc.
To enhance critical literacies	• raised questions and extended students' questions about constructions of gender, race, class, ability, sexuality, and culture in different kinds of texts • encouraged individual inquiry projects with a critical literacy focus
To extend students' capabilities in writing and representing	• worked with students individually and in small groups in the context of their self-generated projects to teach them what they needed to know to complete their projects • used texts created by professionals as exemplars to highlight features of genres and the kinds of decisions that authors make
To teach language conventions	• raised students' awareness of the function of language conventions in published writing or representations by discussing their importance to clarity of message and the impression (positive or negative) on the reader or viewer • instituted regularly scheduled workshops, on specific aspects of language conventions, that students could opt into or attend upon teacher's recommendation

Once the extended investigation was well underway, Todd found that he was spending more time than he had in the past interacting with individuals and small groups. He seemed always to be in motion—listening, talking, questioning, demonstrating, organizing, encouraging, and rethinking. At the outset, he devoted a number of classes to working with the students to establish routines and expectations. The students developed work plans and used individual work folders, in which Todd required them to make brief notes at the end of class, to inform him about what they had accomplished and what they had planned for the next class. He reviewed these notes daily so that he could intervene when necessary to get students back on track. Written conversations through the folders became a very effective way of keeping communication open and of making students accountable.

For the students, the inquiry became an extended exercise in critical literacy as they explored the powerful ways in which texts work in the world and learned to exercise power through their use of language. Todd drew on the work of literacy educators and researchers such as Barbara Comber (2001), who writes about how

> …critical literacies are negotiated in the more mundane and ordinary aspects of daily life. Critical literacies include an ongoing analysis of textual practices:
>
> • How do particular texts work?
> • What effects do they have?
> • Who has produced the text, under what circumstances, and for which readers?
> • What's missing from this account?
> • How could it be told differently? (p. 1)

The students drew upon these questions as they examined multiple texts featuring adolescents. Their analysis generated additional questions about the positioning of different kinds of adolescents and the very real effects this positioning has on young people's lives. African-Canadian male students in the class contested the racism they encounter, often exacerbated by adult mistrust of teens in any shape or form. They talked, wrote, and represented what it feels like to live as a young, black male in North American society. Young women shared their struggles with trying to emulate the ultra-thin young female cultural icons that dominate movies, television, and the music industry. Drawing on their personal experiences and critical analysis, students mobilized and extended their language/literacy capacities to construct a "different account" of adolescence, thus challenging the status quo.

Instructional Focus: Critical Literacy

Todd wanted his students to become more critically literate, but he knew that most of them had little or no experience with looking critically at texts. He introduced critically analytical questions through an examination of the newspaper article that sparked the controversy. Using a copy of the article on an overhead, he guided the students through a step-by-step critical reading of the text.

At the beginning of the year, Todd had oriented the students to group work, but he took the time to review what was expected.

Examining the language and structure of the text

> How does this text work?

Beginning with the headline, Todd asked the students to identify all the words and phrases that described adolescents or adolescent behavior. He wrote the words on the board and asked the students to consider

- Who is the adolescent described? What is he like?

Todd drew the students' attention to how the article was organized.

- What is the writer arguing? How did she or he shape the argument? What ideas are given precedence?
- Did the writer solicit information or opinions from others? How was that corroborating evidence used to support the argument?

Response as readers

> What effects does this text have?

Todd asked the students to respond as readers.

- How do you react to this text? How does it make you feel? What thought does it provoke? How might your parents react/feel/think? Younger children? Community members? Seniors? City council members? Local police?
- What actions might be taken as a result of this text? Who might be affected by those actions?

Reflecting on authorship

> Who has produced the text, under what circumstances, and for which readers?

Todd invited the students to put themselves in the position of the reporter, editor, and publisher of the newspaper.

- Why would they write this text in this way? What do they have to gain? Who was their intended audience?

Reading beyond the text

> What's missing from this account?

Reminding students about the initial heated discussion regarding the article, Todd asked,

- Why were you so angry? What do you know that is not reflected in this text? What's missing?

As the students offered ideas, Todd recorded them on the chalkboard for reference in completing the final part of the lesson.

Rewriting the text

> How could it be told differently?

In the last part of the lesson, Todd divided the class into groups of four and asked each group to rewrite the article, telling the story differently by drawing upon the ideas about what was missing from the newspaper version. The groups typed up their alternative versions and Todd made overheads so that each group could present to the class, considering the critical questions in relation to the alternative versions. Todd guided the students to understand that no texts are neutral; all texts construct reality from a particular perspective and can only ever be partial accounts.

Meeting the Needs of Diverse Learners

There were several students in the class who struggled significantly with reading and writing. Despite Todd's efforts to provide high-interest texts at their instructional level, they would not read anything that looked like a book used in school. These students were just as interested as the others in the topic of adolescents, however, and wanted to be part of the collective inquiry. In response, Todd and the resource teacher worked collaboratively to structure experiences with which these students could experience success. The teachers built on the students' familiarity and comfort with media and electronic texts, extending their capacities to comprehend, analyze, and construct using digital cameras, video equipment, and computers. The teachers gradually introduced graphic novels and short print texts, providing instruction on reading strategies to help students gain access to these texts. Over the course of the inquiry the students became more confident to tackle complex texts, having developed more flexible and strategic approaches to reading.

Assessing for Student Growth

Todd was aware of the research (Black et al. 1998) that demonstrates the powerful positive impact of student-involved assessment on student achievement.

As a teacher of students completing their last year of high school, Todd believed strongly that students should take responsibility for self-assessment, thus learning an essential life-skill. Therefore, while he was actively engaged with the students as they engaged in assessment of their learning, he placed major responsibility on them. When he realized that the students' investigation was going to constitute the curriculum for the semester, he set aside time in class to discuss with them how they, together, were going to ensure that students met provincial achievement expectations. He also outlined his own classroom expectations, providing guidelines for how students would engage actively in a number of ongoing assessment activities and provide evidence of their achievement at the conclusion of the semester.

Translation of Achievement Expectations

Todd made copies of the provincial achievement expectations for Grade 12 English language arts and engaged students in translating them into language that was more descriptive and concrete. For example, Outcome 1 in the Alberta Program Outline states

> Students will listen, speak, read, write, view, and represent to explore thoughts, ideas, feelings, and experiences.

The Outline further expands this outcome with specific outcomes related to forming tentative understandings and interpretations, experimenting with language, considering new perspectives, expanding interests, and setting personal goals.

1. Todd asked the students to meet in small groups and rewrite the general outcome in their own words, telling them what it might look like if a student had accomplished what was expected. The students agreed that the outcome meant that they needed to be able use all six language systems effectively for learning. They talked at length about what it means to explore, referring to the specific outcomes for examples of the kind of thinking and learning that should occur.
2. Todd challenged the students to develop a list of the kinds of learning experiences associated with their investigation that might help them achieve the outcome. The students agreed that they would need to engage in personal and critical responses to the texts they were reading, and that they should be willing to take some risks in posing new ideas and using language in different ways. They discussed how important it would be to keep open minds about the perspectives in the texts they were interpreting and analyzing, and to respect each other's points of view. They determined that evidence of achieving this outcome could be reflective writing, self-assessments, teacher observations, and products that demonstrated their exploratory thought.
3. After the students worked through each of the outcomes, Todd compiled and edited the notes from the discussions. He created a two-page handout with the translated expectations and the lists of learning experiences. The students put the handout in their work folders for reference during goal setting, planning, and assessment discussions with Todd. Every two weeks Todd set aside some time in class to revisit the handout as a group to take stock of how they were doing collectively and individually in working toward the achievement of the expectations.

Ongoing Student-Involved Assessment Activities

Student work plans and folders

The students were accountable to Todd for developing and following a work plan and for informing him about what they accomplished each day. He required them to provide evidence of how they were organizing and keeping track of their work. To support this, he offered examples of ways that they could keep records through simple charts or narrative diaries with dated entries. Students could keep their records electronically if they wished, but they were

Todd wanted to encourage the use of technology but, since access to computers was sometimes problematic, it was much easier for him and for the students to jot brief notes in the folders.

required to communicate in writing with Todd through the folders each day. He could quickly review the students' entries and respond at the end of the school day. This regular communication provided him valuable insights into students' learning that he used when planning instruction. For example, a student might write, "Ben and I don't quite know where to go next with this script that we're writing. We've run out of ideas. We need a writing conference with you."

Identification of strengths and needs; goal-setting

After the discussions related to achievement expectations, Todd asked students to complete an assessment of their own strengths and needs in relation to the expectations. What expectations or parts of expectations had they already met? Felt confident they could achieve? Would really require effort and teacher support to accomplish? Seemed totally impossible? Then he met individually with each student during class time, when they were engaged in independent and small-group work, to review their self-assessments, give his input, and help them set goals for the next four weeks. The students commented on their progress towards their goals in the communications through the work folders, and met monthly with Todd.

For most students, the subsequent meetings after the initial goal-setting were brief sessions just to touch base and make revisions for the next month.

Teacher–student conferences

In addition to the conferences for goal-setting and revising, Todd made a point to touch base with each student at least once a week—and more frequently if necessary. During these interactions, Todd asked students to talk about what was going well and where they needed help. The conversations gave him useful information to guide his instruction. He could identify needs that students had in common and plan mini-lessons, for small groups or for the whole class. Todd encouraged students to identify for themselves when they needed his help and to think about what kind of help they needed. There were also conferences related to work in progress, such as drafts of writing or a storyboard for a video production.

Such conferences took place throughout the work time, with and without Todd, as students became more used to helping each other.

Critical self- and peer-assessment of evolving products

As the products of students' inquiries began to take shape, and students worked towards refining them for a public audience at the exposition, Todd engaged them in critically reflecting on the evolving work. He asked students to meet in small groups to share their work in progress. In preparation for the discussion, the students completed individual critical self-assessments in which they responded to the following questions:

- How do you envision the final product of your work?
- What information, ideas, themes, or questions are you trying to explore or communicate?
- What do you consider the strengths of your work in progress?
- What more do you anticipate doing?
- How do you hope an audience will respond to your work?

In the peer-review sessions, each creator presented the work in progress and the responses to the questions, inviting comment and input from members of the group. These reviews helped students clarify how best to move forward, having received feedback from an audience of peers.

Providing Evidence of Achievement

Portfolios

As part of the work with translating provincial expectations, Todd discussed with students how he proposed to determine if they had achieved the outcomes by the end of the course. He introduced the idea of a "status report portfolio" (Stiggins, 2001) in which each student would compile evidence to demonstrate accomplishment of each of the outcomes. He emphasized that the evidence would differ from student to student, depending on their prior experiences and the nature of their contributions to the collective investigation. Students would need to annotate the items included, explaining how the evidence demonstrated achievement. They would also need to write a final reflection on the learning to submit with the portfolio. As the semester advanced, Todd used both class time and conference time with individual students to help students work on their portfolios.

Public Exhibition

The students' public exhibition of their work was another means of providing evidence of achievement. The final products put on display reflected the quality of the students' learning and thinking. Todd asked each student to complete a self-assessment that included reference, not only to the final product, but also to contributions made to the processes of planning and executing the event. Todd also made observations related to participation, and assessed each final product based on a rubric that he and the students developed.

Involving Parents and Community

Because the curriculum that evolved in Todd's classroom was quite different from what parents themselves had experienced and what they expected from a high-school English course, he sent each parent a letter, describing what the class was doing and how students were meeting curricular expectations. He and the students developed a link to the school website that described the genesis of the project and showed examples of work in progress. At mid-semester parent-teacher meetings, Todd discussed the project and shared evidence of students' work. He extended an invitation to students to be part of these conferences and about half of them participated, leading the discussion related to their work folders and offering their perspectives on the project.

The exhibition at the conclusion of the investigation provided an opportunity for parents and the wider community to see what the students had accomplished and to become better informed about adolescents. Those who attended commented on the quality of the products on display and on the thoughtfulness, creativity, and engagement of the students. School-board officials told Todd how impressed they were with the students' insights into their own learning and their ability to talk knowledgeably about what they had achieved. The feature article in the community newspaper offered readers a different story from the usual

By the end of semester, when Todd used the portfolios for summative assessment and for grading, he was quite familiar with each student's work, and could work through the portfolios fairly quickly.

reporting about teenagers. For Todd and the students, the exhibition provided public confirmation of what they already knew—together, they had learned to use language effectively to have an impact beyond the classroom. As Comber (2005) puts it, they learned how to use "language and other symbolic resources to get things done in the world" (p. 5).

From Fighting to Friendship in Grade 3

It is perhaps not much of a stretch to imagine that a group of young adults about to leave high school are capable of self-directed learning and critical literacy. But what about younger children? Many elementary-age children are just as able as are their older brothers and sisters to grapple with how the world works. Teachers committed to making connections between literature, literacy, and life can enact that kind of curriculum in Grade 3—and even earlier— if they are responsive to what children are trying to tell them.

Nadia Singh had never before met a class quite like her Grade 3. In her fifteen years in teaching she had not encountered such a diverse and difficult group of students of any age. She was not so concerned about their broad range of academic needs; she was used to responding to many different kinds of learners. What had caused her to lose sleep was the constant arguing and lack of good will that pervaded a classroom that was anything but the harmonious community she wanted to create. Nadia had a reputation for being able to handle anything and had successfully managed difficult classes in the past. This time it was different; none of her usual approaches seemed to make much difference.

As she observed the children over the first month of school, she became aware that there were several tightly knit cliques, each of which came from a different community. Much of the bickering seemed to stem from competition and disagreements between these groups. As well, she was disturbed by the subtle—and sometimes not-so-subtle—bullying of children who didn't seem to fit anywhere. Most of these children came from the poorest neighborhood served by the school. Two of them were African-Canadian and one was bi-racial. Nadia found it interesting and a bit puzzling that a couple of the in-groups included African-Canadian and South Asian children; the impact of race on the social relations within the class was obviously complex. There was a lot of name-calling and rough play aimed at the loners. She noted that the children who were the brunt of the teasing and bullying avoided contact with others at recess, and always seemed to be left out. In the classroom, when given a choice, students opted to interact and work with their usual friends, only reluctantly accepting "outsiders" when Nadia formed groups.

One morning late in September Nadia gathered the class in a circle and said, "I think that our class has some problems that we should talk about." She went on to describe what she had observed and invited the children's comments. One of the most popular boys protested, "Well, we can't be friends with everybody." Nadia countered, "So, if someone is not your best friend, does it mean that you should fight and argue with them and not include them in games at recess? Do you think there might be different kinds of friends? Do you think anyone can have too many friends?" In the lively discussion that ensued, children talked about their notions of friendship and getting along, and the problems that sometimes arise.

As she listened and interacted, Nadia began thinking about how she could address the relationships among the children through the curriculum. She had been planning to begin reading a novel aloud to the children and to introduce them to literature circles, using sets of books that she had available. She also wanted them to choose their own books to read independently. She decided that she would tackle the relationship problem through engagement with literature. From her classroom shelves and the school library, she collected as many texts as possible related to friendship and getting along, and displayed them in a prominent place in the classroom.

The next morning she told the children that she had been thinking about the conversation of the day before. She said it seemed to her that it would be helpful in solving the problem within the class to find out more about how people get along with each other as friends, classmates, neighbors, and community members. She began by leading the children through a brainstorm on "What is a friend?" Then she divided the children into small groups, making sure that members of each of the cliques were distributed across the groups, and asked them to develop a list of qualities that they look for in a friend. In debriefing the small-group discussion, Nadia highlighted the similarities across groups and discussed with the children how most of us want the same kinds of things from our friendships. She then drew the children's attention to the books on display, picking a few to show and talk about briefly. Before the morning ended, she gave the children a chance to browse the books, and concluded with a challenge to the children to add to the collection.

Over the next six weeks, the children's language-arts program focused on the ever-expanding collection that included picturebooks, novels, poetry, non-fiction, and comics. Nadia showed several films and engaged the children in exploring what their favorite TV shows revealed about relating to peers. The children responded to their reading through discussion, writing, and the visual arts. They wrote stories and poems about relationships. The class explored the problems that often occur between friends, both in real life and in fiction. They read and discussed stories in which unlikely friendships evolved between people who seemed very different or who initially did not like each other. From time to time, Nadia engaged the children in role-playing in which they worked through scenarios about getting along. Throughout all the learning experiences, she posed questions that encouraged children to make connections with the problematic relationships within the class.

The children raised questions and issues that led to productive investigations of difference. One little girl commented that she thought girls were better at making friends than boys. Her remark sparked conversations about whether boys' and girls' friendships are different, and took the children back to the texts to see in what ways stories reflect gender differences in the nature of friendships. The children read stories set in a variety of cultural and historical contexts, and reflected on similarities and differences with their own experiences. Nadia talked about moving to Canada as an immigrant at the age of nine and the difficulties that she experienced fitting in when she went to a classroom of strangers in a new country. She invited children to talk and write about times when they went into unfamiliar situations and had to make new friends.

Through the learning experiences Nadia offered, the children gained new insights into people and relationships. Because she structured the classroom to promote interaction across the existing cliques and to include those who had been isolated, children learned about each other and discovered common experiences and interests that connected them. Three little boys who had not previously played together found that they shared a passion for comic books. When reading a story about friendship set on a ranch, a group of girls who were besotted with horses discovered that one of the new girls they had marginalized had lived on a farm and learned to ride when she was three. Nadia smiled when she saw the once lonely little girl laughing and talking with her new "horsemates" on the playground.

At the conclusion of the six-week exploration, Nadia asked the children to reflect upon what they had learned and how their classroom had changed as a result. The children wrote and talked about how much better they knew all their classmates, about new friendships that were forming, and about how much more fun it was in the classroom without everyone fighting with each other. The experience reaffirmed Nadia's belief in the power of literature to transform ideas, feelings, beliefs, and social relations. Although the children's engagement with literature—deepened through talk, writing, and the arts—was crucial to bringing about changes in the classroom culture, it was not sufficient. It was Nadia's thoughtful and reflective teaching that helped children connect literature with their lives, and thus grow—both as people and as language users.

Consider This

As you reflect on this scenario, consider the parallels with Todd's experiences with his Grade 12 students.

1. How would the role of the teacher be the same and different in this earlier grade?
2. What kind of literacy instruction might Nadia have incorporated?
3. How might she have handled assessment and ensured that children accomplished expectations?
4. How might she have involved parents and community members?

Bibliography

Allen, Janet. (2000) *Yellow Brick Roads*. Portland, ME: Stenhouse.

Allen, J. (ed.) (1999) *Class Actions: Teaching for Social Justice in Elementary School and Middle School*. New York, NY: Teachers College Press.

Allington, R. (2001) *What Really Matters for Struggling Readers: Designing research-based programs*. New York, NY: Addsion-Wesley.

Anderson, M. & Dousis, A. (2006) *The Research Ready Classroom*. Portsmouth, NH: Heinemann.

Bigelow, B. & Peterson, B. (eds.) (1998) *Rethinking Columbus*. Milwaukee, WI: Rethinking Schools.

Bigleow, B., Christensen, L., Karp, S. Miner, B. & Peterson, B. (1994) *Rethinking Our Classrooms*. Milwaukee, WI: Rethinking Schools.

Black, P. & Wiliam, D. (1998) "Inside the black box—raising standards through classroom assessment" *Phi Delta Kappan*, 80 (2), 139–148.

Black, P., Harrison, C., Lee, C., Marshall, B & Wiliam, D. *Assessment for Learning: Putting It into Practice*. Buckingham, UK: Open University Press.

Blair, H. A. & Sanford, K. (2004) "Morphing literacy: Boys shaping their school-based literacy practices" *Language Arts*, 81 (6), 452–460.

Bomer, R. & Bomer, K. (2001) *For a Better World: Reading and Writing for Social Action*. Portsmouth, NH: Heinemann

Booth, D. (2006) *Reading Doesn't Matter Anymore…*Markham, ON: Pembroke.

Charlton, B. C. (2005) *Informal Assessment Strategies*. Markham, ON: Pembroke.

Christensen, L. (2000) *Reading, Writing and Rising Up: Teaching about Social Justice and the Power of the Word*. Milwaukee, WI: Rethinking Schools.

Comber B. (2005) *Literacies with Currency: Teachers work to make a difference*. Keynote Address. Austalian Association of Teachers of English/Australian Literacy Educators Association National Conference. Gold Coast, Queensland AU, July 1–4.

Comber, B. & Cormack, P. (1997) "Looking beyond 'skills' and 'processes': Literacy as social and cultural practice in classrooms" *Reading: A Journal about Literacy and Language in Education*, 31(3), 22–29.

Comber, B. & Simpson, A. (eds.) (2001) *Negotiating Critical Literacies in Classrooms*. Mahwah, NJ: Lawrence Erlbaum.

Comber, B. (2001) "Negotiating critical literacies" *Schooltalk*, 6(3), 1–2.

Cornett, C. & Smithrim, K. (2001) *The Arts as Meaning Makers*. Toronto, ON: Pearson.

Cornett, C. (2007) *Creating Meaning through Literature and the Arts*. Toronto, ON: Pearson.

Daniels, H. (2002) *Literature Circles*, 2nd ed. Portland, ME: Stenhouse.

Davies, A. (2000) *Making Classroom Assessment Work*. British Columbia: Connections Publishing.

Dewey, J. (1938) *Language and Experience*. New York, NY: MacMillan.

Evans, J. (2005) *Literacy Moves On*. Portsmouth, NH: Heinemann.

Flesch, R. (1985) *Why Johnny Can't Read*, 2nd Ed. New York, NY: Harper and Row.

Goodman, K. (1967) "Reading: A Psycho-linguistic guessing game" *Journal of the Reading Specialist*, 6, 126–135.

Goodman, Y., Watson, C. & Burke, C. (1987) *Reading Miscue Inventory*. New York, NY: Richard Owens.

Graves, D. H. (1983) *Writing: Teachers and Children at Work*. Portsmouth, NH: Heinemann.

Graves, D. H. (2002) *Testing Is not Teaching: What should count in education*. Portsmouth, NH: Heinemann.

Hansen, J. (1987) *When Writers Read*. Portsmouth, NH: Heinemann.

Harste, J., Woodward, V.A. & Burke, C. (1984) *Language Stories and Literacy Lessons*. Portsmouth, NH: Heinemann.

Harvey, S. & Goudvis, A. (2000) *Strategies that Work*. Portland, ME: Stenhouse.

Harvey, S. (1998) *Nonfiction Matters*. Portland, ME: Stenhouse.

Kajder, S.B. (2006) *Bringing the Outside In*. Portland, ME: Stenhouse.

Kohn, A. (2000) *The Case Against Standardized Testing: Raising the scores, ruining the schools*. Portsmouth, NH: Heinemann.

Kucer, S. (1991) "Authenticity as the basis for instruction" *Language Arts*, 68, 532–540.

Lake, J. (1997) *Lifelong Learning Skills*. Markham, ON: Pembroke.

Leu, D. J., Jr., & Kinzer, C. K. (2000) "The convergence of literacy instruction with networked technologies for information and communication" *Reading Research Quarterly*, 35, 108–127.

Luongo-Orlando, K. (2003) *Authentic Assessment*. Markham, ON: Pembroke.

Matters, G. (2001) *The Relationship between Assessment and Curriculum in Improving Teaching and Learning*. Paper presented to the national ACACA conference. Sydney, AU, July.

Mcmackin, M. & Siegel, B. (2002) *Knowing How*. Portland, ME: Stenhouse.

Mead, S. (2006) *The Evidence Suggests Otherwise: The truth about boys and girls*. Washington, DC: Education Sector. Retrieved June 27, 2006 from http://www.educationsector.org

National Council of Teachers of English Statement on Multi-modal Literacy. Retrieved June 1, 2006 from http://www.ncte.org/edpolicy/multimodal

National Council of Teachers of English/International Reading Association. (1996) *Standards for the English Language Arts*. Urbana IL/Newark DE: NCTE/IRA.

Newman, J. (1984) *Whole Language: Theory in use*. Portsmouth, NH: Heinemann.

Newmann, F. & Wehlage, G. G. (1995) *Successful School Restructuring: A report to the public and educators*. Madison, WI: University of Wisconsin, Education Center.

Ohanian, S. (1999) *One Size Fits Few: The folly of educational standards*. Portsmouth, NH: Heinemann.

Ontario Ministry of Education (2004) *Me Read? No Way!* Retrieved January 12, 2006, from http://www.edu.gov.on.ca

Paterson, K. (2006) *Real Life Literacy*. Markham, ON: Pembroke.

Rowsell, J. (2006) *Family Literacy Experiences*. Markham, ON: Pembroke.

Shelton, N. & Fu, D. (2004) "Creating space for teaching writing and for test preparation" *Language Arts*, 82(2), 120–128.

Skiffington Dickson, D., Heyler, D., Reilly, L.G. & Romano, S. (2006) *The Oral History Project*. Portsmouth, NH: Heinemann

Smith, F. (1883) "Reading like a writer" *Language Arts*, 60(5), 558–567.

Smith, F. (1971) *Understanding Reading*. New York, NY: Holt, Rinehart & Winston.

Smith, F. (1978) *Reading Without Nonsense*. New York, NY: Teachers College Press.

Smith, M.W. & Wilhelm, J. D. (2006) *Going with the Flow*. Portsmouth, NH: Heinemann

Stead, T. (2001) *Is That a Fact?* Portland, ME: Stenhouse.

Stead, T. (2005) *Reality Checks*. Portland, ME: Stenhouse.

Stiggins, R.J. (2004a) "New assessment beliefs for a new school mission" *Phi Delta Kappan*, 86(1), 22–27.

Stiggins, R.J. (2004b) *Student-involved Assessment for Learning*. Upper Saddle River, NJ: Prentice-Hall.

Vasquez, V. (2003) *Getting Beyond "I Like the Book"* Newark, DE: International Reading Association.

Weaver-Hightower, M. (2003) "The 'boy turn' in research on gender and education" *Review of Educational Research*, 73, 471–498.

Wilhelm, J. & Edmiston, B. (1998) *Imagining to Learning*. Portsmouth, NH: Heinemann.

Wydro, K. (1981) *Think on your Feet: The Art of Thinking and Speaking Under Pressure*. Princeton, NJ: Prentice-Hall.

Index